BORN BAD

CREATION BOOKS

LONDON, ENGLAND

Credits

BORN BAD
by
Jack Sargeant
ISBN 1 871592 62 3
A Creation Book
First published 1996
by
CREATION BOOKS
London, England
Copyright © Creation Books 1996
World rights reserved
Creation True Crime – a periodical publication
Photographs by courtesy of:
Associated Press
The BFI
The Jack Hunter Collection
Thanks to:
Eric Miller

British Library Cataloguing in Publication Data.
A catalogue record for this book is available from the British Library.

CONTENTS

CONTENTS

BORN BAD

Foreword

Born Bad consists of two essays commissioned especially for this volume by Creation Books. The first essay, *From Nebraska To The Heart Of Darkness*, tells the story of Charles Starkweather and Caril Ann Fugate, the two blue denim love-struck killer teens who would do anything to defend the magic of their own special world. This essay was written in close collaboration with Jack Hunter, who provided the necessary research materials, and advised on the text. All quotes from Charles Starkweather are reproduced verbatim.

The second essay in this book, *Gun Crazy*, focuses on the cultural impact of the Starkweather and Fugate story, and primarily its impact on dominant modes of cinema. This essay attempts to delineate a cinematic sub-genre which, in part, has been motivated by the themes and issues raised by the case of Starkweather and Fugate. This sub-genre includes such cult films as *Badlands*, *Kalifornia*, and *Natural Born Killers*, which are comprehensively analyzed and compared in this section of **Born Bad**. Once again this essay was written in close collaboration with Jack Hunter.

Acknowledgements:

The following people assisted in the completion of this volume: Jack Hunter, James Williamson, Peter Colebrook, Stephanie Watson and Mark Waugh.

Introduction

In the 1950s America ruled the world, fully emerging as a global power. Under Dwight D. Eisenhower, who was elected in 1953, the country began to change. On the outskirts of towns suburbs began to grow, while television began to create a national culture. Emerging from this cultural change was the teenager; a new moneyed group intent on spending their money and time enjoying themselves. The entertainment industry soon recognized the economic potential of teenagers and by the mid-'50s films and fashions began to be specifically targeted at this new market. In 1956 Elvis Presley appeared on *Toast Of The Town*, a program which was hosted by Ed Sullivan and counted nearly a third of the population among its viewers: fifty four million people. As much as it launched Elvis, and teen culture, the show offended social groups and churches nationwide, all of whom feared a rebellious wave of libidinal juvenile delinquency which would threaten the very fabric of society.

But, beneath society's fear of rock'n'roll rebellion, of juvenile delinquents who raced cars and cussed, lurked a far more real force. A tortured figure who believed that he was "numbered for the bottom". Like a black mirror he reflected the fears of society back at it; distorting and magnifying them, mutating them. His name was Charles Raymond Starkweather.

Fear Rouses Countryside
With Multiple Killer Abroad

Bennet, Neb.— Terror stalked the countryside Tuesday night. Farm houses became armed camps and grim-lipped men and women here, 16 miles southeast of Lincoln, burned lights far past the usual bedtime.

There was only one conversation topic – a gun-crazy teenage murder suspect and his 14-year-old girl friend.

Where would Charles R. Starkweather, 19, strike next?

Was his girl friend, Carol [sic] Fugate, a willing accessory, dead herself or accompanying the youth out of terror?

Authorities working around the clock said there is no doubt the stubby, green-eyed youth with a shock of red hair worn in a popular teen-age style is responsible for the six killings.

"All our deductions add up to the same answer," said Lincoln Police Chief Joe Carroll. "Starkweather is our man. I just hope he doesn't kill anyone else."

"Never in my 27 years on the force have I seen anything to compare with these wanton murders," Mr. Carroll declared.

"That goes for me, too," said Assistant Chief Eugene Masters. "There can't be any other answer."

Horror mounted in Lincoln and throughout Southeastern Nebraska as dusk fell and the word got around that three more killings had been added to the triple murder discovered in Lincoln Monday.

Volunteer posses were formed.

Off-duty policemen and other law enforcement officers called control points with offers to work around the clock on their time.

In farm houses shotguns, rifles and pistols were taken

from closets and racks and placed in strategic, easy-to-reach places.

Mrs. Conrad Leader, who with her husband operates a filling station here, paused while sounding the 6 o'clock whistle.

"Three-quarters of the men in this town were on the hunt for Carol and Robert [Carol King, 16, and Robert Jensen, 17] all day," she said.

"My husband was among them. No one carried a gun. I'll guarantee you they will all be carrying guns when they go out again."

Herbert Randall, hardware store operator, appeared haggard after his all-day search. He looked at his powerful hands with hard eyes, started to say something and stopped. He walked out of the station.

On the porch of a modest home on a muddy street here, Warren King, 26-year-old brother of Carol, stood with jutted jaw, fighting back tears.

"When she left Monday night she told me she would have Bob bring her home at about 10:30," he said.

"I knew something was wrong when she didn't come home, but I didn't think it was going to end like this."

He said that Carol had been living with him and his wife because their father had died of a heart attack three weeks ago. "And then came this... and then came this!"

Those who knew 70-year-old August Meyer, who was slain on the back porch of his well-kept, white, two-storey farm house, were outraged as well as grieved.

"Augie kept as nice a farm as you will find," said a friend.

"He cared for his mother until she died not too long ago. And then along comes this kill-crazy punk and shoots him."

As the night wore on the lights in the small town and farm houses continued to glow.

No women or children walked the streets.

Terror stalked the countryside.

—*Omaha World Herald*, January 1958

From Nebraska
To The Heart of Darkness:
The True Story of
Charles Starkweather and Caril Ann Fugate

1

Charles Starkweather was born on November 24th, 1938, the third of seven children born and raised in the abject poverty of depression America, to Guy and Helen Starkweather. Charles Starkweather spent much of his childhood living in a "shabby one story structure" a "shack", in the town of Lincoln, Nebraska. Even before his crimes Charles Starkweather was an outcast, literally born as an outsider, his lack of status marked not just by the poverty of his family but also by his physical appearance. Charles had been born with bowed legs, about which he would later write "I believe a pig could run between them without touching the sides". Starkweather also suffered for much of his youth with a speech impediment, as well as chronic myopsis (which remained unrecognized until he was fifteen and had nearly completed his schooling, the result being that – rather than being the academic failure his teachers had mistaken him for – Starkweather had in fact been unable to even see the blackboard, no wonder, then, at the rambling quasi-intelligibility of his confessions). As it was Starkweather appeared somewhat short and stocky, an appearance that did not benefit from his shock of, by 1950s standards, rebelliously long red hair, and the cheap clothes he had to wear. His classmates gave him the derogatory nickname "Red Headed Peckerwood", and even among his, few, friends he was frequently referred to as "Little Red".

In his autobiographical outpouring, aptly entitled *Rebellion* and written during his incarceration, Starkweather described the hatred and humiliation he experienced during his childhood, which he believed began on his first day at school;

"School that first morning... Mrs Mott let everyone play and do what they wanted, I didn't get along that day in school with the others, they made me a little mad but more upset than anything else, they didn't seem to want to have anything to do with me, not let me play with them or anything else and that's the reason I played in the sandbox by myself that first morning, everybody left when I came over to play with them in the sandbox, they'd left went off among some other girls and boys talking about me, because out of corner of my eye, I glanced at them, the girls giggling and boys giving off their snickers, then they wented off occupying them selves to some other simple tasks."

For Starkweather the isolation (whether it was authentic or merely imagined) of this moment, this first contact with both society and his peer group, this initial contact with the world was the moment which affirmed his status as an outsider: "happy times" he would later state "were cut off by the hatefulness"[1]. It was the inauguration of his rebellion:

"My rebellion against the world started that first day in school and from that day I became rebellious. I had stayed in my rebellious mood even to this day. Why had I become rebellious against the World and its human race? – cause that first day in school I was being made fun at, picked on, laughed at. Why were they making fun of me? My speech was one thing and the other was my legs, I was a little bowleged. In those younger years of my life I haded builded up a hate that was as hard as iron and when people tease, make fun of and laugh at a little youngster in hers or his early childhood, that little youngster is not going to forget it. I wouldn't deny I was like a hound prowling for fights, quarrelling, and doing wild things and placing everyone among my enemies. Kids picking on me and not having a thing to do with me caused me to have black moods, at least that is what I called them, cause most of the time, I would just sit in one place and stay motionless in a gloomy manner and it was obvious that there was no reasoning with me when in one of my black mood and Boys and girls that I knew didn't bother me while I was in my motionless and gloomy manner, they would just let me and stay in my Black mood and even to this day I still have them melancholy moods."

Some journalistic reports would later describe Starkweather as a fighter, a child and teenager who would regularly use violence in response to his abusers. This image of Starkweather emerges from *Rebellion*, in which Starkweather wrote:

"The hate that became strong inside of me when I was a youngster by those who were making fun and always teasing me are the ones that started me to fight. I would beat them down and if I had to I would beat them down again until they knew that I wasn't going to take it from them. At times and with the right emphasis my attitude was merely a sparodic outburst, but at other times as I realized now was something thronie, when I was fighting those who picked on me, I fought fast and a little furiously like a mamiac in rage and fury and as I fought sense of outrage grew to striving, to throw, to bend, to hurt and most of all to beat those that teased me, but as I fought the general opion of school kids became particularily that I had a reputation for meanness or generosity."

But, if Starkweather saw himself as having "the reputation for doing nothing but fighting" others, including his neighbours, teachers and childhood associates would later remember a different Starkweather. Rather than a fighter they saw a young man who was quiet, and perhaps even shy – especially around girls – a teenager whose school 'citizenship record' revealed a pupil whose behaviour was considered to be above average.

If Starkweather was a victim at school, then the few aspects of his home life which have emerged reveal a similar alienation in the form of chronic poverty. When viewed against his physical 'disability' and his humiliating social relationships at school then his poverty must also be viewed as a marker which served to separate Starkweather from the community; these elements all serve to emphasize his state of 'outsider-ness'. In *Rebellion* Starkweather is revealed as acutely sensitive, not just to the taunts of his fellow students but also to his family's low social position and poverty; as Starkweather put it: "poverty gives you nothing. People who are poor take what they can get". For Starkweather poverty was a trap, he could map its confines, and trace its borders, but Charles could see no escape from it for himself; if he remained the model of citizenship that his school believed him to be, "it would be the same thing all over again". He believed that his very life was rigidly controlled: he saw that he would not be able to flee the bludgeoning poverty which had characterized his working class childhood but instead would be condemned to repeat it, eventually finding himself a manual job, a wife, having children and then simply dying.

If much of *Rebellion* has been read and interpreted as an example of Starkweather's imaginary exclusion from the realm of the social, and his tales of school are viewed as either youthful exaggeration or perhaps over-sensitive, this sense of injustice to his family's plight and his certainty of his own poverty, is certainly both factual and understandable.

Starkweather: "What did not make this world a good place to live in was that nobody cared about me for what I could do. They hated me because of the way I looked, and because I was poor and had to live in a goddamned shack; it didn't matter what we all loved each other; that my mother worked hard away from home to help support us children, and washed our clothes and cooked and got us off to school. All these goddamn kids cared about was 'What kind of job does your old man have? What kind of a house do you live in? What do your legs look like? Are you taller than any girl in school?'"

2

Charles Starkweather may have felt alienated, but his youthful interests were comparatively similar to those of most teenagers growing up in the American Mid-West in the '50s. He had a fondness for comics, particularly the violent EC horror and crime comics, and the B-movies which would play at Lincoln's cinemas; Starkweather reserved a particular fondness for westerns and horror movies. Like many other teenagers he enjoyed the thrill of hot-rodding, and was the proud owner of a 1949 Ford, which he had carefully stripped down, converting into a hot-rod which he was occasionally known to drag. Starkweather had one passion that was greater than cars, however; he was an able huntsman, having learnt the necessary weapons skills from his father:

"Dad was an exspert at handling firearms and by following his instructions and watching him, I learned the so call safety measures that had to satisfy dad before he'll permit me to carry and use a firearm. It is true that I have always been an out door sportsman, firearms beside automobiles, and beside that of my family, have been my ruling passion, but between the firearms, and automobiles, I rather hear the crack of a firearm than have or drive the finist car in the whole wide world."[2]

In 1956 James Dean appeared as the archetypal disillusioned teenager in Nicholas Ray's film *Rebel Without A Cause*. A film

---

which depicted an existentially confused group of teens, set against the backdrop of a middle class family melodrama. Despite the differences in class Starkweather immediately identified with the rebellious figure (at least by '50s standards) of James Dean. After seeing *Rebel Without A Cause* at the local drive-in Starkweather began to idolize Dean, and began to emulate his appearance and posture (the entire fixation must be read as somewhat ironic, given that Starkweather had a series of very good reasons to be a rebel). Unfortunately Starkweather lacked the financial resources to buy and wear new clothes and he was thus forced to wear thrift store and hand-down clothes, his cheap cowboy boots, emblazoned with a blue and white butterfly design, were several sizes too large and he was forced to stuff them with strips of crumpled newspaper in order to wear them without them slipping from his feet. Similarly his second-hand clothes made him feel that he was wearing the "skin of a dead man". Feeling increasingly alienated, he believed that he was wearing clothes which had previously been worn by the very people who mocked and hated him.

If the stories of his violent behaviour at school are in dispute, and may be interpreted as products of his own over active imagination and perceived sense of exclusion, as his peer group would later testify, then some details of his youth would appear to be contradictory. Starkweather was forced to change schools due to his delinquent activities, which included fighting, and hot wiring cars in order to go joy riding when his own hot-rod was not available. Starkweather was forced to transfer to a new school at the beginning of the ninth grade.

At this new school Charles Starkweather immediately came into contact with a similar juvenile delinquent, a greaser named Bob Von Busch. The bow-legged, red-haired Starkweather was immediately a target for Bob Von Busch's bullying and Busch attacked Starkweather. The fight ended in a draw: the two teenagers recognized that they were evenly matched. From this moment on Starkweather and Von Busch were inseparable, and they became the best of friends. Bob Von Busch was dating Barbara Fugate and soon Starkweather was introduced to Barbara's fourteen-year-old sister Caril Ann Fugate. Despite being only fourteen years old Caril Ann Fugate was already known in her neighbourhood, Belmont, for her sexy, rebellious attitude; the perennial appeal of 'jail bait'. The couple's first outing was a double date with Bob and Barbara to the cinema, as Bob would later recount; "we went to the movies a lot, the drive-ins mostly"[3]. The first date was successful and Caril and Starkweather immediately became close, and the two couples would regularly double date.

Starkweather's previous experiences with the opposite sex were, at least according to Starkweather's accounts, unsatisfactory. Certainly Starkweather dated girls, "I went out with girls, some were mild dates with nice Christian girls, but most of the girls I went out with, were either the gibberty gibbit type, that used too much make-up, and dressed in expensive clothes, or they were the harlot type, that weren't hard to get a date with, and easy to get along with." However for Starkweather these girls were – at least in his eyes – unsuitable, he felt that they were either unsuitable because of his poverty, or that they were not the type of girl "a kid gets along with". Exactly what it took to "get along with" Starkweather was ambiguous, although he would later tell his prison psychologist James M. Reinhardt that the one "nice girl" he dated "got to upsetting my death deal". It was 1957 when, in the fourteen-year-old Caril Ann Fugate, Starkweather found a girl friend who was willing to participate in his "death deal".

3

Charles Starkweather and Caril Ann Fugate grew close, and soon Starkweather began to grow jealous of any other male who would show interest in Caril. On one occasion a boy showed an interest in Fugate, but Charles (or 'Chuck' as Caril would call him) grew jealous, eventually threatening the boy with violence if he did not stop pestering Caril.

At the age of sixteen Charles Starkweather decided to leave school, a place which he identified only with the social hierarchy and its manifestations through bullying, fights and misery. The teenager with a James Dean fixation decided to find employment, and was soon working in a local warehouse; loading and unloading trucks carrying paper for the Newspaper Union. It was while working at this warehouse that Starkweather was struck on the head, just above his left eye, by the heavy lever on a machine which he was operating. The blow knocked Starkweather cold, and was severe enough to require medical attention and resulted in Charles receiving several stitches. Charles would later claim that the injury resulted in continual headaches and occasional periods of confusion[4].

If Starkweather thought that school was emotionally draining and characterized by a feeling of profound alienation then he must have found his first full time job equally, if not more, demanding, and demeaning. The men with whom he worked

---

Born Bad

not only laughed at his disabilities, they also considered Starkweather to be stupid, a fact which they believed to have been emphasized by his thoughtless accident with the machine (at his trial his employer at the Newspaper Union, John Hedge, would describe Charles as the "dumbest man who ever worked for me"). Further, the warehouse of the Newspaper Union was rigidly stratified, with every employee knowing his or her place in the deferential chain of command and power. Needless to say the ill educated, uncoordinated teenage school drop out was at the very bottom of the pecking order, forced to do the most unpleasant jobs. Starkweather would later describe his position in the social hierarchy: "They had me numbered for the bottom". Charles' lowly position led him to become increasingly bitter;

"I tried to do work as good as anybody, even done things myself that two of us shoulda done. I used to think: now, no more hating, no more fighting ...then something would happen to take it all out of me. I used to wonder why 'no goods' like some I knowed was getting praised for doing what they done. Guess it's cause they talked better'n I did; cause they had better to places to sleep at night."

Starkweather's experience of continued alienation within the workplace, and the growing relationship with Fugate, who he believed was still being pestered by the teenage boys at her school, led him to give up his job at the warehouse. Starkweather soon began a new job; that of garbage man, earning a very meagre $42 per week. The garbage route was a job with which he was familiar, having worked at it part time during school vacations, and it had benefits; he would finish work before three o'clock when Caril finished school and would be able to devote his time to her. Of course the job had its downside; he had to start work so early in the mornings that it was not even light, and, in addition to this, the job of teenage garbage man was exceptionally poorly paid.

The low income from his new job caused problems for

Starkweather, who had recently stormed from his parental home after a fist fight with his father which ended in his being physically thrown from his parents' home. Like everything else at that point in Starkweather's life the fight concerned Caril, who had recently been in a minor car accident while driving Charles's car, which his father had helped to pay for. Unfortunately Caril did not have a license, as she was still only fourteen years old, and The Lincoln Police Department punished Caril by making her write a five hundred word essay. Guy Starkweather perceived his son's irresponsibility in letting Caril drive the car as an act of obvious stupidity, but the love struck teenager naturally saw it differently. After being forced to leave the relative security of his parents' home Starkweather found himself sleeping on the floor of newlyweds Bob and Barbara Von Busch's boarding house apartment. Soon Charles had his own rooms in the same boarding house, but while having his own space, and finishing work at three, meant he could spend the afternoons making love with Caril, his low income barely covered his basic living costs, and Starkweather soon fell behind in the rent.

Starkweather's poverty, and his realization that, despite working hard, only a "nincompoop would do this dirty work" led him to contemplate ways out of the poverty trap in which he was finding himself. Everyday on his route, collecting the garbage from across town, where the middle and upper classes of Lincoln, Nebraska, lived, he saw what he was being excluded from. Starkweather began to recognize his hatred, often feeling that he wanted to "do something... maybe go out and rob a bank or throw garbage in some old bitch's face", and on at least one occasion Starkweather was reported to have driven the garbage truck through the streets shouting out abuse at the pedestrians as he slowly cruised past. More importantly the alienated teenager began to realize that there was one way out of the hardships and inequalities that defined and controlled his life. While heaving heavy, stinking sacks of trash for a minimum wage Starkweather came to the realization that, for him, there was one great leveller of class, one way in which he would find himself equal with the rest of the society which had oppressed, dominated and alienated him, a method by which he would also find retribution, as he would later state; "dead people are all on the same level".

4

"The more I looked at people the more I hated them... a bunch of goddamned sons of bitches looking for somebody to make fun of... some poor fellow who ain't done nothin' but feed chickens."

"These braggarts and good people are not laughing at a stupid garbage type... they'll have something real interesting to say after tomorrow."

It was below freezing on the night of the 1st December, 1957, when Starkweather drove his Ford to the outskirts of Lincoln to the Crest Service Station. It was three o'clock in the morning and Charles Starkweather was going out to get more than gas. Starkweather had been to the garage the previous day to buy a toy dog, a stuffed cuddly toy, perhaps for Caril's Christmas present. Unfortunately Charles' lack of financial resources meant that he did not have enough money to buy the toy, and to make matters worse when he had asked if he could purchase the cuddly toy on credit the assistant, Robert Colvert, had refused.

The following night, as Starkweather pulled up to the gas station, he tied a bandanna around his face, and armed with his twelve-gauge shotgun, he forced Robert Colvert, the twenty-one-year-old who had refused his request for credit the previous day, to hand over the contents of the cash register. The terrified Colvert did as he was instructed, giving Charles the entire contents of the till: $108.

Starkweather then forced Robert Colvert into the back of his car and drove a short distance to a teenage hang-out just out of town. It was here that teenagers would drive to on dates, their libidos pumped up with hormones, alcohol and – best of all – fear. Local teen mythology had created the legend that out on the edge of the great plains, just past the town's limits, the small house next to the road was occupied by a mad old lady, known to the imaginations of the aroused teenagers as Bloody Mary. The legend described Bloody Mary as an ever vigilant psychopath who would shoot and kill anybody who came within shotgun range of her house which was located on Superior Street. In actuality Bloody Mary was an ordinary old lady who, when pestered by the local teenage population, would load her shotgun with rock salt and 'harmlessly' blast the salt at the youths.

Starkweather brought Colvert to the road near Bloody Mary's house and forced Colvert from the car. Here Starkweather's story becomes confused; as would frequently happen during the court case Starkweather's confessions and court room defence testimony did not necessarily match with the physical and forensic evidence left at the crime scenes. As the two men climbed from the Ford, Colvert attempted to snatch the twelve-gauge from the teenager's hands; in the process of fighting Starkweather cocked the gun. Colvert grabbed the barrel and, as the two fought for possession of the weapon, it discharged, shooting Colvert. "He shot himself the first time. He had ahold of the gun from the front, and I cocked it and he was messing around and he jerked it and the thing went off." The second shot was deliberate, as Colvert tried to stand up Starkweather shot him again, from point blank range, the barrel of the twelve gauge pushed up next to the back of the young man's head. "He didn't get up anymore".

However, when he was finally apprehended and questioned Starkweather initially insisted that he did not actually intend to kill Colvert, but just leave him. This raises the dual questions of why kidnap somebody after a robbery, a gesture which must be viewed as risky, and secondly if Starkweather did not intend to kill Colvert, why did he take him to a place where the murder could be 'blamed' on the mythic figure of the gun toting old lady, Bloody Mary?

5

The following day Charles Starkweather met Caril from school as usual. As they drove over to his apartment he told her he had been involved in the robbery of the Crest Station, although he claimed that somebody else had shot Colvert. Whether or not Caril believed him is disputable, what is certain is that she not only understood his "death deal", she was now a crucial part of it, becoming its motivation and its cause.

"They say this is a wonderful world to live in, but I don't believe I ever did really live in a wonderful world. I haven't eaten in a high class restaurant, never seen the New York Yankees play, or been to Los Angels or New York City, or other places that books and magazines say are wonderful places to be at, there haven't been a chance for me to have the opportunity, or privilege, for the best things in life."

"(I) Don't know why it was but being alone with her [Caril] was like owning a little world all our own... lying there with our arms around each other and not talking much, just kind of tightening up and listening to the wind blow or looking at the same star and moving our over each other's face ...I forgot about my bow legs when we was having excitement. When I'd hold her in my arms and do the things we done together, I didn't think about being a red-headed peckerwood then. We knowed that the world had given us to each other. We was going to make it leave us alone..."

Caril Ann Fugate understood Charles' sense of alienation and outsider-ness, and, with Charles' debts paid and cash to spare, she willingly shared in a fantasy world with him. While a massive manhunt spread through the town and suburbs of Lincoln, as well as the surrounding countryside, Fugate and Starkweather spent the afternoons in Starkweather's apartment. Here they would make love, practice knife throwing, sing and dance to records, and sometimes they would plan for their future. Chuck spent the $108 on presents for Caril. They even drove up to the Crest station on the outskirts of town, just so that Charles could buy Caril that stuffed toy puppy that she loved so much. Legend has it that the couple saw every film in town and danced to the plastic 45s that made up the hit parade. Charles had money, and for a brief hiatus, life was good to the teenage couple. Then the money began to run out.

6

The relationship between Charles Starkweather and Caril Ann Fugate's parents Marion and Velda Bartlett (Marion was Caril's step-father) was never easy. Early on in his relationship, when it was apparent to everybody that Starkweather was in love with the young Caril Ann Fugate, he had asked her parents if they would consent to his marrying Caril. Caril's parents were less than keen on the idea of their fourteen-year-old girl marrying the bow-legged outsider and forbade them to marry. Starkweather and Fugate were forced to wait until Caril reached the age of majority. While most couples would have kept quiet if placed in this position, Charles had decided that he would tell his work mates at the warehouse that he was getting married anyway, regardless of the truth or the inevitable consequences.

A short time after starting this rumour Starkweather started another: he was going to be a father, his fourteen-year-old wife was pregnant. This rumour spread throughout the community like wildfire, and caused some dissent with Caril's teachers and, perhaps understandably, shocked and upset her parents. Charles did not care, he gave up his job at the warehouse to become a garbageman.

A few months after starting these rumours, and six weeks after murdering Robert Colvert, Charles Starkweather found himself broke again. His landlady, Mrs May Hawley, padlocked him out of his apartment, and had thus temporarily shut the door on the special little world which he had shared with Caril for little over a month. It was a cold winter, and Starkweather was forced to sleep in his car, which he kept in an unheated garage. He slept in his car for a week. Then, on the 21st January, 1956, he borrowed a single shot .22 rifle from a friend, under the pretence that he was going hunting with Caril's stepfather, Marion Bartlett. Although, given that Marion Bartlett had heard the rumours Charles had spread about both his marriage to Caril, and her pregnancy, it could be assumed that Mr. Bartlett probably did not want to go hunting with Starkweather. But, of course, Starkweather also had ulterior motives for travelling to the Bartletts' residence at 924 Belmont Avenue, in the blue collar area of Belmont, to see the Bartlett's that morning.

Charles Starkweather entered the home of Marion and Velma Bartlett and their daughters Caril Ann Fugate and Betty Jean Bartlett, aged two and a half, and – according to his testimony – he began to show Velma a series of carpet samples and cuttings he had found on his garbage route. Mrs. Bartlett was less than interested in Starkweather's rubbish bin carpet samples. Charles then asked her if her husband was ready to go hunting, to which she replied in the negative. Starkweather wanted to know why Marion was not ready to go hunting. According to Starkweather's later testimony Velma said that she did not want him to see Caril anymore[5], a comment which naturally angered and upset Charles and consequently led to a heated confrontation, which climaxed with Velma Bartlett hitting Starkweather: "She didn't say nothing. She just got up and slammed the shit out of me."

After being hit by Caril's mother, Starkweather left the house. However he returned a few minutes later and again entered the house. This time he found Mr. Bartlett waiting for him and the two began to argue. "The old man started chewing me out. I said to hell with him and was going to walk out through the front door, and he helped me out. Kicked me right in the ass. My tail hurt for three days." His pride and ass hurting Starkweather sped off in his car, pulling over by a telephone box in order to phone Marion Bartlett's work and inform them that Marion was ill.

Following the phone call Starkweather drove to a relative's house and parked his car in the drive. Then, on foot, he walked back to the Bartlett's house and sat and waited on their back porch for their daughter to return from school. Starkweather knew when Caril would be returning from school because her dog, Nig, would begin to bark in the front garden. Shortly after hearing the dog's bark Starkweather heard Caril and her mother "yelling their heads off" from inside the house, as Caril's parents angrily argued with their daughter about her apparently delinquent red-headed boyfriend.

Starkweather stood up from where he had been waiting on the porch and entered the house through the back door. As he walked into the house Velma accused him of getting Caril pregnant, and attacked him once more. "She got up and slapped the shit out of me." This time, however, Starkweather was ready; "I hauled off and hit her one back", despite the fact that Starkweather claimed that he slapped Velma Bartlett rather than punched her he admitted that the blow was heavy enough to have "knocked her back a couple of steps". Immediately after striking Mrs. Bartlett, Starkweather was again attacked by Caril's father. Marion picked Starkweather up and began carrying him "by the neck" to the front door. However this time Charles Starkweather had nothing to lose and he put up a vicious struggle, kicking Mr. Bartlett ("somewhere", Starkweather would later claim). The two men fell to the floor, and Mr. Bartlett ran out of the room. Charles assumed that Bartlett had run off in order to grab a weapon, and began to load the rifle he still had with him.

Marion Bartlett burst back through the door, running at Starkweather with a claw hammer in his hands. Charles Starkweather raised the rifle at Caril Ann Fugate's stepfather and pulled the trigger. The shot hit Bartlett in the head and

---

he collapsed. Immediately after this Velma Bartlett came at Starkweather with a kitchen knife raised in her hand. Starkweather would later say that she was shouting that she was going to "chop my head off". Before Charles could do anything Caril had grabbed the barrel of the rifle and was trying to snatch the weapon from Charles, not because she wanted to save her mother, but because she wanted to kill her mother herself, she wanted to "blow her to hell". Velma pushed Caril to one side and came at Charles, but Starkweather still had the rifle in his grasp and "just turned around and shot her". The bullet from the rifle hit Velma Bartlett in the face, seriously wounding but not killing her outright, but such was her momentum that she continued to move, past Starkweather towards her youngest daughter Betty Jean. As she arrived next to Betty Jean she stopped. Starkweather thought that she was going to pick up her daughter, but she did not, "she just turned around and looked at me again". Starkweather responded to Velda Bartlett's stare by hitting her with the rifle's butt, Velda fell down, but was still not dead, so Starkweather hit her again with the heavy gun butt, this time Velda did not move: "she just laid there".

Starkweather then turned his attention to Caril's half sister, who having just watched her parents being killed, was crying hysterically. The teen killer now had mayhem scorching his nerve-endings. Starkweather – having just finished clubbing Velda with the gun butt – hit Betty Jean Bartlett with it. Betty Jean fell against a table, and began to scream. Caril then told Charles that her step father was not dead but only wounded. Charles then began to walk into the room where Marion Bartlett still lay, picking up the kitchen knife, that he had been threatened with by Velda, on the way. Meanwhile the infant Betty Jean continued to scream. Charles Starkweather: "the little girl kept yelling, and I told her to shut up, and I started to walk again [towards Marion], and just turned around and threw the kitchen knife I had at her". The hours of practice knife throwing paid off for Starkweather; the knife hit Betty Jean in the throat, although Charles believed he had actually hit the screaming two-year-old in the chest. Having killed the bawling child Charles resumed the task at hand. "I went on in to the bedroom. Mr. Bartlett was moving around quite a bit, so I tried to stab him in the throat, but the knife wouldn't go in." In order to force the knife into the flesh of the man's throat Starkweather raised his hand and, slamming his weight into a blow at the knife's handle, forced it deep into Marion's throat. In order to be sure that Marion Bartlett was dead Charles Starkweather proceeded to stab him several more times in the throat. Then watched and waited to make absolutely sure the man was dead. Following the murders of Caril's family, Charles re-loaded the rifle, and sat down to watch television. "I don't even remember what was on. I just wanted some noise. It was too quiet." Charles would remember. Charles found murder hungry work, and as they watched television the two young lovers ate sandwiches, which Caril had prepared.

Having stabbed, shot and clubbed three people to death, they had left the house in some mess. Starkweather and Fugate began to clear up, wiping blood from the floors and walls then removing the corpses. The heavy corpse of Marion Bartlett was dragged outside to the chicken coop behind the house. Here Charles and Caril hid the bloody cadaver beneath a collection of rags and fading old newspapers. Velma Bartlett's body was first wrapped in bedclothes before being carried to an abandoned outhouse behind the Bartletts' residence, here Charles forced Caril's mother's body down into the toilet hole in the outhouse. The woman who had forbade him from seeing Caril, who had slapped him, was pushed into an old toilet. Young Betty Jean's body was placed inside a small box, and was also carried to the abandoned outhouse, where the box was placed on top of the toilet hole.

Caril Ann Fugate and Charles Starkweather then settled down to six days – barely a week – of playing house. In order to stop inquisitive visitors Caril hung a sign on their front door which read "Stay a way Every Body is sick with the Flue". Despite the presence of this sign there were several visitors during the six days. The first was a school friend of Caril's who came on the morning of the first day of simulated 'domestic bliss', calling to ask if Caril would walk with her to school. On that first cold Nebraska morning, Caril told the young girl that she had the flu, and was sick. The ruse worked and the girl walked to school by herself; it did not, however, deter her from calling again, every morning of the week. Neither Caril nor Starkweather even bothered to open the door to the girl on these subsequent mornings. The milk man would come by each day, and Caril would purchase milk and bread each day on credit. Charles would go into town and buy food. He also brought Caril a series of presents including a puppy and a collection of records.

One morning Marion Bartlett's employer, along with a fellow employee, knocked on the door. The two men were coming by in order to see if Marion Bartlett was fit enough to return to work, but Caril – who by now was quite the actress – told them that her step father had the flu and was not well enough to return to work. The two men believed the girl and went away. Later in the week Barbara and Bob Von Busch came to visit Barbara's family. Once again Caril would not let anybody into the house, again pointing to the crudely scratched sign tacked onto the front door. Barbara's and Bob's suspicions were aroused by Caril's acting. Later that same day Bob returned, this time bringing Charles' brother, Rodney Starkweather. This time Caril changed her story, no longer telling the callers on the doorstep that her family had flu. Instead Caril – apparently tearfully – told her brother-in-law and Rodney Starkweather that they must leave, and could not come in, because, if the did not go, her mother's life would be in danger. Exactly why Caril changed her story remains unknown, although it would later be a defence offered by her lawyers. Their suspicions aroused Bob Von Busch and Rodney Starkweather immediately went to the police. The police decided to pay a visit to the Bartlett house in Barlow.

The police went to the Bartlett residence, but when Caril opened the door to them she merely reiterated her original story and pointed at the sign. When the police inquired about her refusal to let her relatives enter (for some reason believing her flu story, despite the fact that this was not the story that she had told Bob and Rodney) Caril stated that she would not let them into the house because Barbara had a new born baby, and that she did not want the young child to catch the flu. The police then asked why Bob would have come to them over this matter, and Caril merely shrugged, telling the two officers that they would be better off asking Bob why he had turned to them. She then stated that she felt that Bob did not like her, and was persistently worried about things anyway. Incredibly, the police believed the fourteen-year-old-girl, and went away.

Finding the police response unsatisfactory Bob and Rodney decided to send a friend of Caril's to the house. The friend was turned away by Caril who offered a third excuse as to why she could not let anybody enter the house: Chuck, and a friend of his, were in the house, armed with a machine gun; Caril was being held hostage. Having heard this story the friend went away, but instead of reporting back to Bob and Rodney she told her father the story. He did nothing until the following day when he notified the police. It was Monday.

Also on that Monday morning Caril's grandmother came to the house. The elderly Pansy Street was worried about the rumours of goings-on and the flu story emanating from her daughter's house. Caril told her grandmother that if she did not go away, Mrs. Bartlett would be hurt. Pansy Street immediately went to the police, who by now had also heard the story of Caril being held hostage. The Lincoln police sent an officer around to the house to investigate the stories. But he arrived to find an empty house, and decided that Pansy Street was just being nosy and interfering.

If the police did not believe anything suspicious was transpiring, then the Von Busch's and Starkweather's were becoming increasingly concerned. Not only was Caril offering a series of different stories to visitors, stories which shared only the narrative of refused entry to the Bartlett house, but Charles had also gone missing, and nobody had seen him for a week. Finally Bob, Rodney and Pansy convinced the police to investigate properly. Later that day Pansy Street and two officers returned yet again to the Bartlett house. They knocked several times. Nobody answered their blows on the door, so, ignoring the badly scrawled flu sign, they decided to enter the house. A cursory glance revealed that the house was empty. Charles Starkweather and Caril Ann Fugate had realized that their 'honeymoon' was over, and had blown through, packing a few meagre belongings into Starkweather's car and leaving town.

Within a few hours Bob Von Busch had located the whereabouts of his murdered in-laws. Suspicion fell on the two missing teenagers, and the Lincoln Police and Guy Starkweather decided to issue a warrant for Charles' arrest on suspicion of committing the murders.

7

Charles Starkweather's and Caril Ann Fugate's getaway was less than perfect. Starkweather's Ford hot-rod was in less than perfect condition, and one of the tires was damaged. Charles drove to his rented garage and repaired the tire, and the two teenagers left town. Sixteen miles out of Lincoln, in the town of Bennet, Starkweather and Fugate had to pull over, the engine was not turning over as it should, and Charles' urgent – and thus only cursory – repair of the tire was already failing, and it was nearly flat. The couple pulled over for repairs, and to refill the tank, at a small garage in Bennet. When the police later found out that Starkweather had been spotted sixteen miles away, and heading further away from Lincoln they became increasingly suspicious that Starkweather was not just a suspect but was actually the murderer they were hunting for.

Starkweather was an enthusiastic huntsman, and would regularly drive out of Lincoln, to the surrounding countryside in order to shoot. One regular place he would go to in order to hunt was the farm of an old Starkweather family friend, August Meyer. The seventy-two-year-old August would let Charles Starkweather hunt on the proviso that whatever Starkweather shot he would divide equally, sharing the bounty of the kill. On leaving Lincoln Charles and Caril decided that their best bet to avoid capture was to head for Meyer's farm, which lay approximately twenty miles away from Lincoln, and just outside of Bennet.

It was 27th January, 1958, and – despite being bitterly cold – the winter snow was beginning to thaw, turning the ground wet. August Meyer's small farm lay at the end of a mile long track, which had until recently been covered by a layer of snow and ice, but with the recent thaw it had transformed from a dirt track into a combination of cold, oozing mud, slush and snow. Given the condition of the 'road' it was almost inevitable that Charles Starkweather's hot-rod, which was designed predominantly for town driving, weekend cruising and the occasional game of chicken, with its hurriedly and thus ill-repaired engine, as well as its by now near flat tire, would become stuck in the quagmire that had once been the track to the farm.

Despite pushing the trapped car, and racing the engine, Starkweather and Fugate were unable to free it from the thick mud in which it was entombed. After a number of unsuccessful attempts to free the car the couple resigned themselves to walking to the small farm house. As they neared the farmhouse Caril elected to remain standing on the track (or so she would later claim in court) while Charles walked onto the porch of the farm house. The old man met Starkweather on the back porch, here Charles told August that the car was stuck in the mud and asked him if he would help to pull the car from the mud using his horse. At this point Starkweather's defence and the evidence begin to take separate routes. According to Starkweather and Fugate, August Meyer emerged on the back porch and was angry with Starkweather, the two argued because, as Starkweather would later state, "he couldn't understand why I got stuck there. He thought we should have gotten stuck up closer to his house". Starkweather then claimed that Meyer walked off the porch, back into his house, in order to collect his coat. However instead of putting on his coat the seventy-two-year-old man emerged with a rifle, and attempted to shoot Starkweather, but inexplicably missed ("I felt the bullet go by my head" Starkweather would state). Rather than trying to shoot

Starkweather again the old man turned his back on Starkweather, who just happened to be carrying his rifle. As the old man turned to re-enter the house Starkweather shot him, "at almost point-blank range with the sawed off .410" (a shotgun Starkweather had liberated from the Bartlett residence). But, of course, like the killing of Robert Colvert, Starkweather would argue that August had attacked him, and that in shooting the old man he was actually defending himself.

Caril Fugate would later state that her position on the track meant that she did not hear the argument, but, from her vantage point, she did see her boyfriend shoot the old man. Starkweather would later claim that "Caril got pissed off because we got stuck. She said we ought to go up and blast the shit out of him because he didn't shovel his lane. I said it, too". Already Starkweather's testimony appears to be contradictory; did the old man attempt to shoot him? Starkweather's self-defence argument is possible, but seems extremely unlikely given that August Meyer was a family friend, whom many would later recall was actually close to Charles, further it was Starkweather, not Meyer, who walked onto the porch armed. Or – as the evidence appears to suggest – did Starkweather shoot August for the simple reason that he had been inconvenienced because the track leading to the farm house had turned to mud?

Starkweather then carried Meyer's body to an out-building a short distance from the farmhouse; here he covered the corpse, whose head had been turned to mush by the blast from the .410, with an old blanket. As Charles carried the corpse to the out building August Meyer's dog began barking and ran towards him. Starkweather raised his rifle and shot the dog. He then returned to the house, where he and Caril shared a meal of jam and cookies. They then searched the house, stealing a meagre $100 and Meyer's .22 rifle. The two teenagers then went to sleep.

After allowing themselves a short sleep Starkweather and

Fugate walked back down the track to where their car was still embedded in the mud. They again tried to free it, digging the mud with a shovel they had taken from Meyer's house, but they were still unable to move the car. While they were trying to dig the car free a neighbour of August's, and fellow farmer, drove by in his truck. Seeing the two teenagers frantically digging in the mud he pulled over and offered to help them tow the car out of the mud. Starkweather and Fugate gratefully accepted, and soon the car was towed out. Starkweather thanked the farmer and gave him $2 for his time and help.

The car freed, the couple drove up to Meyer's farm via a different route. This time they did not get bogged down in the snow and mud. As they parked next to the farmhouse Charles ran to the out building where the body of Meyer lay in order to check it. He was shocked to see that the blanket which he had covered the body with had been removed, and, thinking that the body had been discovered he ordered Caril back into the car and they drove back onto the main road. After a short frantic drive they stopped at a road side café in order to eat and more fully consider their situation. Starkweather was already coming to the conclusion that the blanket could have been moved by the wind, and that it was unlikely that the corpse could have been discovered. After a brief discussion the two teenagers decided that they should return to what they considered the safety of Meyer's farm. Inexplicably they decided to drive up the original route and, once again, they became trapped by the thick mud.

This time Caril and Charles did not bother to attempt to dig the car free but instead they left the Ford hot-rod imbedded in the clay-like earth. Then they gathered up their two shotguns and walked down to the main road, where they held the shotguns close to their legs so they could not be seen, then stuck out their thumbs and began to hitch.

8

Starkweather and Fugate were soon greeted by the sight of a car, which they managed to flag down. The young couple – both residents of the small town of Bennet – who were driving in the car were the antithesis to the two denim-clad, shotgun-carrying hitchers. Seventeen-year-old Robert Jensen and sixteen-year-old Carol King, were engaged to be married. Both were popular and successful high school students, and together Jensen and King represented the very social world from which Fugate and, especially, Starkweather felt alienated.

Jensen pulled the car over, and Starkweather asked the driver if he would give them a lift to the nearest telephone, presumably on the premise that the reason that they were hitching was that his car was stuck in the mud. Jensen obliged and Starkweather and Fugate climbed into the car. As the car began to drive Starkweather pushed the barrel of the shot gun into Jensen's neck, and demanded that the couple hand over their money. After taking their money he ordered Jensen to drive the car back, towards the Meyer farm. At the bottom of the track leading to the farm was an old storm cellar, which belonged to a demolished school house at District #79. As they approached the track Starkweather demanded Jensen stop the car by the disused storm cellar.

Starkweather forced the couple from car and down the steps

---

which led to the storm cellar. As they were walking down the steps Starkweather shot Robert Jensen, firing six shots into the left side of the student's head, little realising that in doing so he was signing his own death warrant. Later, in a testimony similarly to his previous murders, Starkweather would claim that his motivation for shooting Jensen was self-defence.

While the description of the shooting of Robert Jensen was comparatively clear cut, the events leading up to, and immediately following, the murder of his fiancée are harder to ascertain, primarily due to the contradictory statements that Caril Ann Fugate and Charles Starkweather would issue at the time of their initial questioning immediately following their arrests, and later versions offered in discussion with the legal authorities during their subsequent trials. All that is certain is that when the two bodies were discovered the following day, by a local farmer called Evert Broening, Jensen was laying face down in a large pool of congealed blood, exactly where he had fallen following the force of the shot gun blasts to his head. Lying on top of Jensen's bloody corpse was the body of Carol King. Like Jensen, King had been killed by a shot to her head; however the sixteen-year-old's body was half naked, with her jeans and underwear pulled down to her ankles, and her jacket and top hitched up around her face and neck. Her exposed abdomen was smeared with mud and blood, and she had been repeatedly stabbed in the abdomen and genitals by an undiscovered sharp object. An autopsy later revealed that one of the stab wounds inflicted on her genitals penetrated the vagina, cervix and rectum; however the autopsy did not reveal the presence of semen.

The testimony which Starkweather would come to offer regarding the murder of Carol King was contradictory, and he changed it several times between his original questioning and his actual trial. Initially he claimed to have spent fifteen minutes with her in the cellar, presumably ordering her to strip for him, and said that he killed her because she began to scream. Later, however, Starkweather changed his testimony, stating instead that, following his killing of Jensen, he had returned briefly to Jensen's car, leaving Caril to watch King. When he returned from the car he found that Caril had shot and killed King. In response to this Starkweather took Caril's rifle and sent her to wait in the car. He then considered raping King and had consequently pulled off her clothes, however the bitter January cold had kept him from being able to maintain an erection and he had thus left her body and returned to the car, which he set about checking. However, Caril Ann Fugate, believing that Charles had raped King, left Charles while he checked out the car and went back to the school storm cellar and savagely hacked at the body of the other woman in a fit of jealousy. An alternative theory posits Starkweather as the perpetrator of the mutilation carried out on King, suggesting that, because of his inability to rape King, he exorcised his sexual frustration with the violent stabbing[6].

Charles' April 9 letter concerning the matter to County Attorney Elmer Scheele would later read as follows:

> i will not claime in this letter to you, on the nurder of Miss king why i'm telling what happened and who shot her. this will tell the truth and the part in what Caril fugate did. but i will be convicted for what i did and thats o.k., but i'll be dan if i want to be sentenced for something i did not do!
> this is how is happened when i shot Bob he drop on the steps and landed on the floor, the girl did not run, i said for her to stay where she was, and i gone on in the cave, he was noveing, so i went up out of the cave, the girl was right where i left her. i went to the car caril f was standing in front of the car, but this time she was in the front seat with the 4:10 out the window with the gun pointing to the king girl. i fill the 22 and got a flash light and went back to the cave, while i was down there i got scared and ran back up and told the King girl to go down i think she was shock cause i had to take her by the arn to get her started. id din't wake for her to get in the cave, i ran to the i was so dan scared i drove off the road. it's in the statement what happen then, to when i begin agin.

we walk up to the cave and told her to come on out, she come out slow so caril pull her up alnost off her feet, i gave the 22 to caril f and said to keep a eye on her, i went on back to the car, i was jacking the car body up to get broads under the wheel, i heard a shot and ran back to the cave, the King girl was right where i left her befor when caril was there. Caril said that the King girl was running and shot her. Caril went into the cave. "the rest is in the statement i gave" we go to the car out about a 1½ hr's later we walk back to the cave and i put the door on the opening and a frane of a window, caril put some broads on it. 2 long ones and sone little one's "when King and bob was in the car heading for the cave Caril f. ask me "if, i already ask the boy for his money yet" in then words "i said no, show then i ask him for it. the nan that got killed in Wyoming. he was asleep when i got there, the door was lock so i yell at hin and he got up. we talk about taking his car so i yell at hin and he got up. we talk about taking his car and he said "no" show i shot two times into the window and then said OK. he started the motor, to let the window down, then he unlock the door and open it then somehow he got hole of the gun and were fighting right in the front seat of the car, i believe i shot hin 2 or 3 tines befor the gun stop work "jamb on me" i call caril to get the orther gun when i looked out the window she was standing behind the car already with the orther 22, i put ny gun from the nans and ran round to the front of his car, when i got to the orther side, (after i shot hin he had a hell of lot of fight left in him) cail ran round the back of his car and began shoting him, "he was yelling something to her while she was shoting away there about having a wife and some kids, and caril said that to back" i didn't the rest of what she said to hin, she was calling hin about every nane below gods sun while shoting him. then she got nad about the blood on the sewat and wasn't going to seat there." there's a lot more i could say but i'n running out of paper." i wish now

i told this in my first statement. caril fugate was the
trigger-happy person i every seen.

Caril's official statement, made to Chief Deputy County
Attorney Dale Farnbruch on February 2nd, went as follows:

D.F: Then what happened when you were walking toward
Bennet?

C.F: Well, there was a car coming around a curve. We had
walked about mile or two, I'm not sure. There was a
car coming around the curve and he stopped him.

D.F: Who stopped who?

C.F: Well, the car coming around the curve, and the car
stopped. I don't know whether he flagged him down
or not.

D.F: Then what happened?

C.F: And we got in the car.

D.F: Both of you got into the car?

C.F: Yes, and the boy said he would take the guns, and Chuck
assured him they weren't loaded.

D.F: Then what happened?

C.F: Then we started off, and started to go to Bennet, and he
asked what was wrong, and he said that the car had
got stuck about a mile back, a little ways back. Then
he asked him which way he was headed toward.

D.F: Then what happened, Caril?

C.F: Then we started going over there, and Chuck pointed the
gun at him and told him to keep going.

D.F: Then did he keep going?

C.F: He said – he told him to keep going or he would blow his
head off. I think that's what he said. The boy said, you
wouldn't do that, or I don't think you would do that,
and Chuck said, do you want to find out buddy. He
said something about buddy, and then the boy kept
driving.

D.F: Then what happened, Caril?

C.F: Then he told him he was going to take his car.

D.F: Where were you going then?

C.F: Going out to Mr. Meyer's place again.

D.F: Was that before or after you had driven on through Bennet?

C.F: After, when we started out to Mr. Meyer's.

D.F: In other words, you were turned around again and going toward Mr. Meyer's farm?

C.F: Yes.

D.F: What did Chuck tell him again, Caril?

C.F: He told him he was going to take the car.

D.F: What did the driver say?

C.F: He said he didn't care.

D.F: What did you say?

C.F: I didn't say nothing.

D.F: And then what happened, Caril?

C.F: And then the boy said he had to be careful, because the car pulled; when we slowed down and stopped the car pulled over to the right, and he told him all about the car.

D.F: Then what happened, Caril?

C.F: Then we started back again to Mr. Meyer's.

D.F: Did you have a gun in your hands at that time?

C.F: Yes.

D.F: Which gun did you have in your hands?

C.F: My dad's.

D.F: Then what happened, Caril?

C.F: Then we started back to Mr. Meyer's and pulled up in the drive. We didn't pull all the way because we got stuck before.

D.F: And what was it stopped near?

C.F: What do you mean?

D.F: Well, was it stopped near anything? Is that where you got stuck before?

C.F: Yes.

D.F: And is that near the cellar?

C.F: Well, the cellar is a little ways off.

D.F: What happened when the car was stopped?

C.F: Well, he told him to get out.

D.F: Who told who to get out?

C.F: Chuck told the boy to get out, and I pointed the gun at the girl. I put it on the back seat and told her to get out.

D.F: You mean you pointed the gun at the girl and told her to get out?

C.F: Yes.

D.F: Why did you do that, Caril?

C.F: Because he told him to get out.

D.F: He told the driver to get out?

C.F: He told them both to get out.

D.F: Then what happened, Caril?

C.F: Then they started walking back toward the cellar, and I got out of the back and got in the front.

D.F: Then what was the next thing you saw?

C.F: I saw all of them go down in the cellar.

D.F: And how long were they all down in the cellar?

C.F: Oh, about a half hour, or an hour.

D.F: Then what happened, Caril?

C.F: Then they started down the cellar and I heard two shots.

D.F: They just went down the cellar?

C.F: Yes.

D.F: And you heard two shots as they were going down in, is that right?

C.F: Yes.

D.F: It could have been more?

C.F: Yes.

D.F: And what were you doing all that time?

C.F: I was just sitting in the front seat of the car.

D.F: Were you watching for anyone?

C.F: No.

D.F: You were just sitting in the car?

C.F: Yes.

D.F: And what happened, Caril, after those shots?

C.F: Then Chuck went down into the cellar. I don't know how long he stayed down there, about a half hour.

D.F: Then what happened after he came up?

C.F: Well, he put the door over.

D.F: Over what?

C.F: Over the top of the place.

D.F: Over the top of the cellar?

C.F: Yes.

D.F: Then what happened, Caril?

C.F: Then he came back and got into the car and started to back out and backed the whole side of the car off in the ditch.

D.F: Then what happened, Caril?

C.F: Then we got out and started getting out.

D.F: Now Caril, before we go any further, let's go back to the time just before you got this car from this driver and this girl and boy were shot. Was there anything else taken from them?

C.F: Yes, there was $4.00.

D.F: And how did that come about?

C.F: Well, Chuck asked them if they had any money, and the boy said yes, he had $4.00, and handed his billfold to Chuck, and Chuck handed his billfold and the boy's billfold to me. I took the money out of the boy's billfold and put it in Chuck's, and handed Chuck's billfold back to him, and handed the boy's billfold back to the girl, because she asked me to.

D.F: Were those the only items that were taken from the boy and girl, the automobile and the money?

C.F: Yes.

Regardless of the 'truth' of any of these contradictory statements, Starkweather and Fugate now had a new car, and – in one day – had added three more names to the growing list of their victims.

9

Charles and Caril now had a new car and they began to make plans for their escape from Nebraska. Initially they decided that they would leave the state and head for Washington, where they believed that they could stay with Starkweather's brother, Leonard. But Starkweather, stating that the car was not running properly, and that he felt tired, turned the car around when they got to the town of Hastings. Instead of stealing another car, or sleeping where they were, they decided to return back to the only 'home' either of them had known. Back to Lincoln.

The first thing they did when they returned to Lincoln was to drive through town to the Bartlett residence, to see if the bodies of Caril's family had been discovered. As they reached the house they saw that parked in front of it were several police cars, and the property was encircled by police officers. The couple carried on driving past the house, and headed up to the "wealthy Country Club section of town". Here they parked the car and soon fell asleep.

On the following day, January 28th 1958, it was reported that Starkweather's Ford had been spotted, stuck in the mud by August Meyer's farm. In response to this sighting of the wanted man's car, Sheriff Merle Karnopp and several officers went to Meyer's house. After a verbal warning to Starkweather the police officers fired several tear gas canisters

---

through the window. These elicited no response and, weapons at the ready, the officers kicked the door down, and entered the farm house. After a brief search of the property the officers discovered the corpse of the farmer who had once been Starkweather's friend. Within a few short hours the bodies of Robert Jensen and Carol King were also found. Two hundred officers and volunteers began to scour the countryside around Bennet and Lincoln.

The sun was just rising in Lincoln, and while twenty miles away Karnopp and his men warily approached Meyer's farm, Starkweather and Fugate were just waking up from a cramped night's sleep in Jensen's car. On awakening the two decided to look for a suitable house in the wealthy district of town. Despite his outsider status Starkweather was familiar with the bourgeoisie district of Lincoln, having worked on the garbage routes in the area. He also knew many of the residents from occasional unskilled odd jobs he would do in the neighbour-hood (primarily yard clearing and small – simple – pieces of repair work). As the sun rose over the town, the two teenagers debated which house would best serve their needs, and which house would make the most suitable target.

Eventually Caril Ann Fugate and Charles Starkweather decided on the house of a wealthy Lincoln-ite, C. Lauer Ward, the president of the Capital Steel Works and a close friend of the governor. The forty-seven-year-old Ward had just left for work, but when Charles and Caril appeared on the doorstep at eight-thirty the door was opened by the Wards' maid of twenty-six years, Lillian Fencl. The fifty-one-year-old, deaf maid let the two teenagers in immediately, unaware that by doing so she was signing her own death warrant. As they entered the Ward residence Starkweather forced the maid to sit at the kitchen table at gun point.

Clara Ward, Lauer's forty-six-year-old wife, was upstairs preparing herself for the day ahead. When she came downstairs she was forced to sit down at the kitchen table by Starkweather. Clara Ward told Charles that she would cooperate with him. While the lady of the house and her maid were kept under guard by Caril, Charles began to explore the Ward house. To the ill-educated, myopic, bowlegged James Dean fan who had spent his entire life in poverty the size of the house and its – at least by Charles' shack childhood standards – lavish interiors were both seductive yet simultaneously repulsive; representing that from which he had always been excluded. After exploring the household Starkweather returned to where the hostages were and demanded that he be served pancakes in the Wards' library. It was not, however, the maid who Charles wanted to prepare and serve him the pancakes, but Clara Ward. As she brought the pancakes in for Starkweather, he would later state, "I decided I wanted a waffle", the lady of the house was thus compelled to return to the kitchen and prepare a different meal for Starkweather. The garbage man had finally managed to force one of the wealthiest residents of Lincoln to wait on him, and had humiliated her by treating her as his servant.

At approximately one o'clock, Mrs. Ward asked Charles if she could go upstairs in order to get a pair of shoes. Starkweather granted the wealthy woman's request and Mrs. Ward went up stairs. Time passed, and Clara had still not returned. After a few minutes Starkweather grew suspicious and decided to go upstairs to find out why Mrs. Ward was taking such a long time. Starkweather began to climb the staircase of the Ward household. As he slowly walked up the staircase Clara Ward stepped out from a room at the top of the stairs, armed – Starkweather would claim – with a .22. Starkweather: "She took a shot at me". After firing Mrs. Ward turned to run but before she could Starkweather, who was holding a knife, "threw the knife at her". The knife struck Mrs. Ward in the back and she collapsed "moaning and groaning", Starkweather pulled the knife from the woman's back, he then dragged Clara into her bedroom. Here Starkweather lifted Mrs. Ward and laid her out on her bed. Before he could complete his task the Ward's pet dog – a poodle – began to annoy him, and interfere with his task. Starkweather picked up the .22 gun and smashed it onto the dog's neck, breaking it and killing the whining pet immediately. He then resumed the task at hand:

"I put the rope around her, or I took a sheet and cut the sheet and put a piece of sheet around her mouth, after that I bound her feet and hands and covered her up."

Following this attack on Mrs. Ward, Starkweather went down stairs and began two tasks which – it could be suggested – were designed to 'justify' his actions. The first was to phone his father. In this conversation Starkweather asked his father to tell his old school friend, Bob Von Busch, that he was on Starkweather's list, and that he was going to be murdered. Starkweather's motive for killing Bob Von Busch, he told his father, was because Bob had attempted to ruin Starkweather's relationship with Caril.

After completing the telephone call, and brief conversation with his father, Starkweather began his second task. This was the writing of a letter, which he addressed to "the law only". This letter was a barely literate blast of psychosis on Starkweather's part[7]. The note was a strangled combination of proclamation/testament/and attempted justifications, all of which found their foundation in the events which transpired the previous week, at the Bartlett household: "nonday the day the bodys were found, we were going to kill our selves but BOB VON BUSCH and everybody would not stay a way", according to the letter, "and hate my older sister and bob for what they are they all ways wanted ne to stop going with chuck snow that sone Kid bob Kwen would go with ne", exactly why the Von Busch's would want to separate the young couple remains questionable, and why would Bob try and find another boy to go out with Caril? Especially considering the fact that the two couples used to double date, as well as the support Bob and Barbara showed to Charles when he needed some where to stay. The letter continued with further tirades against Bob and with the 'Caril' of the letter saying she felt sorry for her sister, because her husband was an ass ("ask"). The narrator of the letter then 'changes' to Starkweather, who wrote "I and Caril are sorry for what has happen, cause I have hurt every body cause of it and so has caril. but i'n saying one thing every body than cane out there was luckie there not dead even caril's sister".

The young couple spent the rest of the afternoon at the Ward household, waiting for C. Lauer Ward to return home. While they waited Starkweather drove the 1950 Ford they had stolen from Jensen into the Ward garage, and drove the Wards' expensive black 1956 Packard into the drive. The couple then loaded the Packard with food, washed and changed their clothes and prepared to leave Lincoln for good.

At six o'clock Mr. Ward returned home. Ward opened the front door to be faced by the short, denim-clad murderer, who was standing just inside the entrance to the house, armed with the .22. Ward was evidently more able to deal with the surprise invasion of his house than Starkweather's previous victims, before Starkweather had a chance to fire the weapon Ward leapt on him and attempted to grab the shotgun. The two men struggled, and Starkweather succeeded in pushing C. Lauer Ward down into the basement. However the force of pushing Ward down into the basement meant that Charles lost his grip on the gun, which also fell down into the basement. Starkweather ran to grab the dropped gun, and as he did so Ward forced his way back up the stairs. Starkweather grabbed the gun and fired a shot, which struck Ward in the back. Ward, although severely wounded and losing blood, was able to continue back towards the front door. He even managed to open it, but before he could step outside Starkweather shot him again, "I was standing about five feet from him, maybe less" he would later recall; from this distance Starkweather was able to shoot Ward in the back of the head. After shooting Ward Starkweather remembered asking him "if he was all right and he didn't answer". Mr. Ward was dead, and Starkweather shut the front door and dragged the bloody corpse back into the house, where he left it just inside the residence. At some point either Starkweather or Fugate also stabbed Mr. Ward in the neck, perhaps to make sure that he was actually dead.

Starkweather and Fugate then turned their attentions to the maid, Lillian Fencl. They took the maid upstairs to a bedroom, and bound her to the bed. Once again the accounts of this murder, and the eventual state of Mrs. Ward's body, were to become a source of dispute between Fugate and Starkweather in court. Starkweather claimed that he did not kill Lillian Fencl, but that Fugate had killed her. While Fugate would state that Starkweather, having tied the maid to the bed, began to stab her and she started "screaming and hollering", necessitating that Starkweather muffle her agony by holding a pillow over her face while he repeatedly stabbed her, Fugate: "every time he stabbed her she moaned". Evidently Fencl took a long time to die, but when she did eventually die the couple covered her body in a blanket.

Regardless of which story was true when the bodies were found the following day, by a business friend of the Wards' who was concerned for their welfare having been unable to contact them, both Fencl and Mrs. Ward had been savagely stabbed to death. Fencl's corpse was found, still tied to the bed, stabbed repeatedly in the chest and stomach, with her limbs similarly slashed. Clara Ward's body was found on the floor of her bedroom, and (contrary to Starkweather's confession that he had only thrown a knife into her back, and just left her in her bedroom tied up and gagged) was similarly butchered, having been slashed at and stabbed in the torso and neck.

Starkweather's full version of events would read as follows:

> that night we stay in the car it was cold but
> we nake I said we was going to have to stay
> somewhere that day cause of the car we had.
> we drove all over thinking what house
> would be the best place to stay show about 8:30 in
> the morning & pick out the one on 24th there was
> two person there they about had a drop dead when

i said we was going to spend the day there.

they said they would be nice and nothing would happen like calling the cops. they were until about 2:00 that after noon the one lady was up stairs and was there about 20 nin i went on up to see her she niss ne about ½" with a .22 cal. gun she just look at ne and back up and begen to run all i had was that knife so it go at her it stop right in her back.

the naid was there i tie her up and left her laying on the beb the dog was there so i had to hit hin to keep bin from barking.

About 6:30 or 7:00 that night the nan cane home i told hin not to nove but he did anyway we was by the basement steps we got into a fight he got the gun fron ne show i push hin doun the basenent steps.

the gun landed on the foor and went off he got and start for it but i frist he pick out iron and i said if i had to c'll kill hin show he lay it back doun i said for hin to walk back up the stairs we was to tie hin up and leave toun.

he start to walk up the stairs he got ½ way and begin to run i shot hin in the back one's the he stop i told hin the next time would be it he got to the top of the stairs and ran for the front door he had it ½ open when i shot hin.

he was laying there naking funny noise i told caril to get a blanket and cover hin up.

we got some food from there and left – last night heading for Washington state we got as far as here when we heard about the fine the bodys of the 3 persons, but weh i lef there was only 1 dead person in that house.

Fugate's testimony:

D.F: Now, Caril, did you go to the Ward house, you and Chuck?

C.F: Yes.

D.F: And was that on Wednesday, or Tuesday? Do you remember the exact date?

C.F: No.

D.F: And who was in the Ward house when you got there?

C.F: Their maid and Mrs. Ward.

D.F: And what did you do?

C.F: I sat down in the chair there, she asked me if I wanted some coffee. Chuck asked me if I wanted some coffee, because the lady asked him. I said yes, and had a cup of coffee.

D.F: Then after you had the coffee, what did you do?

C.F: Then I went and laid down on the couch.

D.F: Where was the couch?

C.F: In the parlor, I guess.

D.F: Now what did you do after you got in there?

C.F: I laid down on the couch and went to sleep.

D.F: How did you sleep?

C.F: I don't know.

D.F: Well, was it for quite a long time?

C.F: Yes.

D.F: While you were laying down there and sleeping, what is the next thing that happened?

C.F: Well, Mrs. Ward brought me – brought some pancakes in to Chuck.

D.F: Did you wake up at that time?

C.F: Yes.

D.F: Did you get some too?

C.F: No.

D.F: And what happened after Charlie ate the pancakes, Caril?

C.F: I went back to sleep.

D.F: And then what was the next thing that happened, Caril?

C.F: Well, when I woke up and I was looking around and couldn't find Mrs. Ward, and he told me that she was dead upstairs in the bedroom.

D.F: Did you hear any shots, Caril?

C.F: No, I didn't, or nothing.

D.F: Was the maid there at the time?

C.F: Yes, she was alive.

D.F: O.K., Caril. What happened after Charles told you that Mrs. Ward was dead upstairs?

C.F: Well, I asked him how he killed her.

D.F: What did he say?

C.F: He said he stabbed her in the throat.

D.F: And what did you say?

C.F: I just said I didn't – well, I didn't say nothing.

D.F: What did he do then after he told you that?

C.F: He had a knife and he told me to go in the bathroom and wash it off.

D.F: Where did you wash it off?

C.F: Downstairs in the bathroom.

D.F: Where was the maid at this time?

C.F: In the kitchen.

D.F: Now, what did you do after you washed the knife off?

C.F: He told me to go upstairs and sprinkle some perfume around.

D.F: What did you do?

C.F: I went upstairs and sprinkled some perfume around.

D.F: After you sprinkled this perfume around and put the bottle back, what did you do then?

C.F: Then I went downstairs, and I think he asked me – I think he told me to go in the closet in the man's room and see if there was any coat or jacket.

D.F: And did you find a coat?

C.F: No.

D.F: Now Caril, did you ever have a gun in your hands while you were in the Ward house?

C.F: Yes.

D.F: And what gun did you have in your hands?

C.F: A .22.

D.F: And was that loaded at the time?

C.F: Yes.

D.F: And what did you do with that gun, Caril?

C.F: I pointed it at the maid.

D.F: And why did you do that?

C.F: Because he told me to.

D.F: You say you were sitting in the living room watching for Mr. Ward.

C.F: Yes.

D.F: Now were you watching for him? What were you looking out of watching for him?

C.F: Out a window.

D.F: And how long did you sit there waiting?

C.F: About a half an hour.

D.F: And where was Chuck at that time?

C.F: I don't know.

D.F: And where was the maid?

C.F: In the kitchen.

D.F: Did something happen?

C.F: Yes, he came home.

D.F: And what did you say?

C.F: I told Chuck he was pulling into the driveway.

D.F: Did you holler at him, or was he beside you?

C.F: I hollered.

D.F: And then what happened, Caril?

C.F: And then—

D.F: Did Mr. Ward drive into the driveway?

C.F: I don't know.

D.F: All right. What happened after you hollered that Mr. Ward was coming?

C.F: I went into the bathroom.

D.F: Which bathroom is that?

C.F: The bathroom downstairs.

D.F: Then what happened as far as you know?

C.F: Well, he told me, then Mr. Ward came home and he didn't get all the way in the house, and I think he said he came in a little ways, in the door, and grabbed hold of the gun.

D.F: Mr. Ward grabbed hold of the gun?

C.F: I think that's what he said, and they started fighting out there, and he was standing by the stairs, and he said he let go of the gun and Mr. Ward fell down the stairs and Mr. Ward started picking up the gun, and he said he picked up the gun, and Mr. Ward, I think he said, picked up a piece of steel or something, and he shot him, I think. I heard a shot. And then he told Mr. Ward to go upstairs nice and easy, and Mr. Ward started up the stairs, and he got a little ways up and started running, and I don't know what happened then.

D.F: Were you in the bathroom all this time?

C.F: Yes.

D.F: What did you see when you came out of the bathroom, Caril?

C.F: Well, the maid was sitting there where the large table is, sitting on a chair there against the wall, and Mr. Ward was laying on the floor by the door, moaning.

D.F: What did you go into the bathroom for?

C.F: I just went in there. I was scared.

D.F: And Mr. Ward, when you came out, was laying by the front door?

C.F: Yes.

D.F: Then where was Chuck?

C.F: He was – I think he was looking out the window.

D.F: And what did he say to you?

C.F: He told me to hold the gun over the maid.

D.F: The .22?

C.F: Yes.

D.F: Let me put it this way, Caril. What happened in relation to the maid then, after Mr. Ward was laying there by the door, and after you had held the gun on her, and he went out to the kitchen and got some food, and then what happened in regard to the maid?

C.F: Well, she sat down there.

D.F: In the kitchen?

C.F: No, in the living room.

D.F: Now then, what happened to the maid after that, Caril?

C.F: Well, before that she was downstairs, and Chuck told her to go upstairs and nothing would happen. When she got upstairs he asked her if she made a phone call and she said no, and he said, if you did, we'll leave, but if she didn't we were going to stay. He said there was supposed to be about fifteen or twenty guys supposed to come, and that's when he told her, he said if anybody came to the door, she would be the first one to get shot.

D.F: In any event, then what happened, Caril?

C.F: Well, then we waited for a few minutes to see if anybody was coming, and then we went upstairs.

D.F: Who went upstairs?

C.F: Chuck, I and the maid.

D.F: Did you have a gun at that time?

C.F: Yes.

D.F: What did you do when you went upstairs, Caril?

C.F: He said for her to sit down in the chair, and I was looking out the window.

D.F: What room were you in at that time?

C.F: One of the bedrooms.

D.F: Then what happened while you were in that room? Was the light on?

C.F: No.

D.F: Did you have anything in your hands other than the gun?

C.F: The light. The flashlight.

D.F: And the maid was sitting in the chair in that bedroom?

C.F: Yes.

D.F: Then what happened, Caril?

C.F: Well, he got a sheet and started tearing it, and then he started to tie her wrist, and I told him why didn't he let her lay on the bed, because she would get tired sitting up all night. I didn't know he was going to kill her then, and then he made her lay down on the bed and started tying her wrists.

D.F: How did he tie her wrists?

C.F: With both hands together.

D.F: And—

C.F: And then he tied them to the bed post.

D.F: Were her hands over her head or not?

C.F: Yes.

D.F: Then what else did he do?

C.F: He tied her feet.

D.F: And did he tie them to anything?

C.F: To the end of the bed.

D.F: And then what happened after that, Caril?

C.F: She kept saying to turn on the light because she was scared of the dark.

D.F: Did somebody turn on the light?

C.F: No.

Born Bad

D.F: Then what happened?

C.F: I was looking out the window, and he started stabbing her, and she started screaming and hollering.

D.F: How many times did he stab her?

C.F: I don't know.

D.F: Did she say anything while he was stabbing her?

C.F: I don't know. He put a pillow over her face.

D.F: Did he stab her more than once?

C.F: Yes.

D.F: Would it be more than twice?

C.F: Yes.

D.F: How do you know that, Caril?

C.F: I heard it. Every time he stabbed her, she moaned.

D.F: About how many times did she moan?

C.F: Well, more than five.

D.F: And then what happened after he got done stabbing her?

C.F: He said he didn't think she was ever going to die, and then he said to shine the flashlight over there and he cut the strips holding her legs, and covered her over.

D.F: What did he cover her up with?

C.F: A blanket that laid on the bed.

D.F: Did you see any blood?

C.F: I seen the blood on the bed, but I didn't see the stabs.

D.F: Then what did he do after he covered her up?

C.F: He told me to shine the flashlight on his arm. There was blood stains all over his shirt; all over the cuff of his shirt.

D.F: What did he do after that, Caril?

C.F: I went and found a white shirt.

D.F: And while you were in the Ward home, did you talk on the telephone?

C.F: Yes.

D.F: And when was that, Caril?

C.F: Just as we started to leave.

D.F: How did you come to talk on the telephone?

C.F: The telephone rang, and I answered it. He told me to answer it.

D.F: Where was this telephone?

C.F: In the kitchen.

D.F: Now, what did you say when you answered the telephone just before you left?

C.F: I think the lady asked how Mrs. Ward was, and I said she was sleeping.

D.F: And then what happened?

C.F: That's about all.

The murders which transpired within the Ward household, as well as the previous murders, led to a massive manhunt for Starkweather and Fugate, with 1,000 police officers, concerned citizens and vigilante searching Lincoln and the surrounding Nebraskan plains. The manhunt was further boosted by the addition on 200 members of the National Guard, who arrived in Lincoln in full cold war apocalypse regalia on the instructions of the state governor Victor Anderson[8] who stated that he had requested the assistance of "all the experienced combat men we can get"[9]. Meanwhile, the town's inhabitants began to live under a growing cloud of terror, each wondering if they would be the next victims of the killer couple's murderous spree.

10

Following the slaughter at the Ward residence Starkweather and Fugate fled in the stolen Packard, heading west, towards Washington, and the dream of living with Starkweather's brother. The couple drove all night, until – by dawn on the 29th January – they found themselves on the border with Wyoming. They stopped near the small town of Casper and spent the seventeen dollars they stole from the corpses at the Ward house on bottles of Pepsi, sweets and petrol. But Starkweather was becoming paranoid that the black car they had stolen from the Wards' house would be too recognizable, especially given that it was being driven by two rebellious looking misfits, hardly the kind of people expected to drive a Packard barely two years old.

While they drove the five hundred miles into Wyoming both Starkweather and Fugate kept their eyes open for a suitable car with which to continue their journey. It was still early when Starkweather spotted what he felt would be a suitably discreet form of transport. A Buick was parked at the edge of the highway, and Starkweather pulled over. Thirty-seven-year-old Merle Collison, a travelling shoe salesmen from Great Falls, Montana, lay slumped across the front seat, sleeping. Charles climbed out from the black car and knocked on the window of Collison's Buick demanding Collison unlock the vehicle and climb out. When the weary Collison refused Starkweather pointed the .22 at the travelling salesman and began shooting. Collison was hit twice in the face, as well as in the neck, chest, both arms and his left leg. His body slumped in the seat, and Starkweather began the difficult task of pulling the bloody corpse from behind the steering wheel.

Starkweather would later describe this shooting, and what he believed was the importance of his final kill:

"People will always remember that last shot. I hope they'll read my story. They'll know why then. They'll know that the salesman just happened to be there. I didn't but him there and he didn't know I was coming. I had hated and been hated. I had my little world to keep alive as long as possible, and my gun. That was my answer."

Unfortunately for Starkweather and Fugate, the shotgun blast had forced Collison's body into a jammed position in the front of the Buick, and consequently Charles was unable to reach the brake in order to free it and start the car. While he attempted to reach and release the brake, and remove Collison's bloody corpse, a car driven by Joseph Sprinkle, a geologist who specialized in searching for oil, saw the stationary car and stopped to offer help, thinking that the Buick and Packard had been involved in an accident. Sprinkle climbed from his car, and as he did so Starkweather turned around, levelling the shotgun at him. Simultaneously to this Sprinkle saw Collison's corpse, from Sprinkle's courtroom testimony:

"I asked 'Can I help you?' He straightened up with a rifle he had behind him and said, 'Raise your hands. Help me release the emergency brake or I'll kill you.' It was then I noticed the dead man behind the wheel. As I approached him, I grabbed at the gun and we fought for it in the middle of the highway. I knew that if he won I would be dead..."

While the two men wrestled for control of the .22 a police cruiser drove past, driven by Deputy Sheriff William Romer. When Romer saw the two men fighting he immediately stopped the car, as he leapt out of the cruiser, Caril Ann Fugate ran towards the deputy. As she ran towards him she shouted out that Starkweather was one of the two men fighting on the highway, that he was a killer, and that she had been kidnapped by him. When Starkweather saw the police cruiser stop he let go of the .22, and jumped into the Packard. The Deputy attempted to open fire at Starkweather, but he was unable to get a clear shot as Caril was running down the road towards him and he consequently would have risked shooting her. Romer pushed Caril into the back of his car and began to chase after the fleeing teenage killer driving the stolen Packard.

Starkweather drove east, heading towards the town of Douglas, Wyoming. As he drove Romer used his radio to call for re-enforcements, and soon Starkweather's car was being chased by several police cars. As the black car entered Douglas it was driving at an estimated speed of one hundred miles an hour. In Douglas people stopped their cars in order to witness the high-speed chase, although their spectacle came to a premature end when they were forced from the main streets by the police shooting at Starkweather's car. The chase soon left Douglas and, on the open highway beyond, began to speed up, with Starkweather's stolen Packard finally reaching one hundred and twenty miles per hour.

Then, as the chase travelled down the highway, one officer shot at Starkweather's car, smashing the rear window. Almost immediately Charles slammed the breaks on and the Packard came to a halt. It was soon surrounded and Starkweather stepped out of the car, his face was sprayed with blood from a small wound near his right ear caused by flying glass from the broken window. Starkweather had stopped the car so quickly because he was under the misapprehension that he had been shot, this sudden surrender prompted one of the arresting sheriffs, Chief Robert Ainsley, to later describe Starkweather as a "yellow son of a bitch". Starkweather may have been a "yellow son of a bitch" but when he climbed from the car, and was surrounded by heavily armed law enforcement officers, he brushed and tidied his shirt – tucking it in – before laying on the ground, despite the fact that the police men were shooting at the ground in front of him and shouting at him to surrender. It was 29th January, 1958, and America's first teenage spree killer was under lock and key.

11

When he was arrested – held at continual shotgun point by Sheriff Earl Heflin – Starkweather was, contrary to police descriptions, the epitome of James Dean-style cool. Once Charles realized that his wound was only superficial, and after he had been handcuffed, he told the arresting officers not to be rough on Caril, as she had not been responsible for what had happened. Charles would later reiterate this claim in a letter to his father, written at the first opportunity following his arrest; "i'm not real sorry for what i did cause for the first time me and Caril have more fun, she help me a lot, but if she comes back don't hate her she had not a thing to do with the killing". Charles, despite initially confessing to all eleven murders, would, at the start of his questioning on February 3rd, plead innocent.

Following the spectacle of his arrest Charles Starkweather was initially incarcerated in Wyoming. However he appealed for extradition to Nebraska. This appeal was soon granted, and on 30th January, the two teenagers were driven, in separate cars and under armed guard, back to Nebraska. Starkweather's motivation in appealing was simple; he had decided that he would rather face the quasi-immediacy of Nebraska's electric chair rather than the slow choking death promised by Wyoming's gas chamber. Nobody felt it necessary to inform the red-headed, myopic, bow-legged teenager that Wyoming's governor was actually against the death penalty and, should the possibility arise that Starkweather was tried and found guilty in Wyoming, he would have almost certainly – had he appealed – received the clemency of a life sentence rather than capital punishment.

Once transferred back to his home state Starkweather was imprisoned in The Nebraska State Penitentiary, while awaiting both his trial and then, finally, on death row. Starkweather was charged with murder in the first degree, which was for the killing of Robert Jensen, the murder of whom County Attorney Elmer Scheele said was confessed by Starkweather in detail. The trial began on 5th May, with much of the legal questions focusing on the question of his 'sanity'. Starkweather's court-appointed attorneys T. Clement Gaughan and William F. Matschullat, attempted to defend Starkweather's murderous spree via the twin discourses of psychiatry and medicine. If Starkweather's criminal behaviour could be explained, if not justified, via these narratives then he would be spared the death penalty in favour of the care of a psychiatric institution. Starkweather's defence thus used psychiatry to 'prove' that Charles was 'insane', and at one stage of the trial one of the defence doctors, Dr John Steinman, stated that Charlie "had a diseased or sick mind". While Dr Nathan Greenbaum claimed that Starkweather was "dangerously sick and is capable of committing dangerous and violent acts".

Starkweather's defence also sought to explain his behaviour as a direct result of a physical abnormality of the brain, whether it was a brain tumour or the ambiguously described "pressure on the brain". These theories were based, at least temporarily on the belief that Starkweather had a damaged eardrum, which his defence decided was either the symptom, or cause, of a brain infection.

For Charles, of course, these defence arguments were antithetical to his actions, to what he perceived were his acts of rebellion. Starkweather would later iterate: "Nobody remembers a crazy man", and for Starkweather his crimes were simultaneously an act of rebellion, and/but also – at least initially – a defence of his life with Caril Ann Fugate. When his defence requested that he submit to medical examinations and an ECG test Starkweather refused, insisting that he was neither suffering from psycho or physiological brain disorders.

Starkweather was insistent that he was sane, and he perceived it as a matter of paramount importance that he be declared such. For his family too Charles' sanity was important, the Starkweather klan did not want to be seen to bare any seeds of madness within their family (it seems strange, when viewed through the therapy infused culture of contemporary society, that the Starkweather family would be less dissatisfied if one of their number was viewed as a murderer than viewed as 'mad', stranger still if madness was such a taboo that Guy Starkweather would spend his days standing outside the courthouse, and later the prison, selling signed photographs of his son). Charles – despite his sense of alienation – did not want to cause any additional suffering to his family (or so he claimed), and this also prompted him to demand the right to be declared as sane. Ultimately, and to the chagrin of Liberals everywhere, Charles knew that his death at the hands of the state, from which he was so profoundly alienated, would be the completion of his actions, as he would later state; "Better to be left to rot on some high hill behind a rock, and be remembered, than to be buried alive in some stinking place". Starkweather also knew that he was "already dead, or [the] same as dead" because "nobody ever gets back hisself again". Starkweather perceived in his death a state of legitimation, the final moment which would transform him into an existential martyr, somebody who would not be forgotten but whose name would live on through the alienation and violence of his life and eventual death. Despite Charles attempts to hinder his defence his lawyers entered the plea of "innocent by reason of insanity".

The prosecution similarly wanted Starkweather to be found, at least in a 'general sense' 'sane', because if found 'insane' he would not be executed. The defence and prosecution both carried out a variety of psychiatric, and quasi-psychiatric examinations on Starkweather, but the results of these tests differed or – more importantly – were interpreted differently. As a consequence of this when Starkweather's defence lawyers claimed that his IQ was that of a near idiot, the prosecution claimed that his IQ – as revealed in their tests – was thirteen points higher. The prosecution psychiatrists found that Starkweather was 'sane', although Dr Edwin Coats eventually decided that Starkweather suffered from a "minor personality disorder". A further prosecution witness, Dr Robert J. Stein – a psychiatrist and neurologist – further described this minor personality disorder as "characterized by emotional instability, considerable emotional insecurity, and impulsiveness... this would fit into a category under the antisocial type of personality disorder". However Stein decided that the teenager was "legally sane" (although exactly how a minor personality disorder may contribute to a serial killing spree seems to be, at the very least, open to question). This minor disorder would, the prosecution argued, not qualify as 'insanity' and if Charles was committed to a psychiatric institution he would soon be released as 'sane', and therefore 'cured'. Such an argument was constructed so that it would play on the both the judge's and jury's consciences and would thus manipulate them into having to find Starkweather 'sane' lest he be freed without having to 'pay for his crimes'.

Starkweather's trial was further complicated by the deterioration of his relationship with Caril Ann Fugate. Following their arrests, and his initial admission of guilt designed and presented so as to protect the fourteen-year-old, the Starkweather/Fugate relationship broke down, undoubtedly due to the pressures of prison and rigorous interrogation at the hands of the law enforcement and psychotherapeutic communities, but also as a result of their psychic separation. When the two teenagers were separated so their own fantasy world – the very world they were trying to protect – began to crumble, and this resulted in the various contradictory statements given by the teens, especially regarding the mutilated appearance of the cadavers of Carol

King, Clara Ward and Lillian Fencl. Once Starkweather became aware that Caril was not just letting him take the rap for the murders but also telling her inquisitors that he had kidnapped her, he began to take a less 'heroic' approach and started to implicate Caril in the slayings, stating that he knew nothing of the violent mutilations of Carol King, Lillian Fencl and Mrs. Ward and suggesting that Fugate had in fact enacted these bloody manifestations of unleashed hatred, and had killed King and Fencl. Starkweather then began to talk even more openly of the murderous complicity of his relationship with Fugate, stating that:

"She could have escaped at any time she wanted. I left her alone lots of times. Sometimes when I would go in and get hamburgers she would be sitting in the car with all the guns. There would have been nothing to stop her from running away. One time she said that some hamburgers were lousy and we ought to go back and shoot all the people in the resturaunt."

Starkweather also wrote more than one letter to the prosecuting attorney directly implicating Fugate in the Jensen/King murders.

The 12 members of the Jury – locals Mrs George McDonald Jr., Mrs Mildred Fagerberg, Ander H. Hallbert, Mrs. Beatrice I. Volkmer, Oliver E. L. Rosenberg, Mrs Adeline E. Muehlbeier, Mrs Evelyn V. Russell, Alvin M. Christiansen, Mrs Ellen E. Heuer, Raymond E. Swanson, Mrs Miriam F. McCully and John Svoboda – took less than twenty-four hours to find that the stocky, red-headed teenager standing before them in a rebellious slouch, was guilty of first degree murder, and, on May 23rd the Jury specified that Charles Starkweather should pay the supreme punishment for his crimes, and demanded the death sentence. As Starkweather observed at the time of his conviction; "I don't think they tried me for Jensen. They tried me for the whole thing."

Following the verdict, and the setting of the date for

---

execution on December 17th[10] – which was delivered by District Judge Harry Spencer on June 7th – Starkweather was taken to the Nebraska State Penitentiary once more. It was here that he would spend the remaining months of his life, primarily devoting his time to writing his autobiography, *Rebellion*, and executing a series of drawings and paintings which reveal a degree of competence. During his period of incarceration (totalling seventeen months from the time of his arrest) Starkweather's murderous psychology became of interest to the prison psychiatrist, James N Reinhardt, who conducted a series of interviews with the teenager totalling some thirty hours. Reinhardt stated that throughout all of these interviews he never saw Starkweather feel any real remorse. However, given that Starkweather knew that he would be found guilty and executed, and his profound alienation, it does not seem surprising that the denim-clad teen did not show any 'real' remorse. Reinhardt was also somewhat unfair in his description of Starkweather's ruthlessness, while Starkweather never fully recanted, in *Rebellion* he did offer a quasi-warning:

"I determined... that I would write these thoughts and rememberences down. For I wanted to do something for my parents. I had caused them enough trouble. And I wanted to warn other boys so they wouldn't take the road I took".

And so Starkweather goes on, a rambling apology suggesting that children attend church and school. Starkweather writes under the guise of a born-again Christian suggesting that he no longer feels the "rebellion toward anything or anyone". Maybe Starkweather was saved, but given the nature of the rest of Starkweather's confessions, and the manner in which he would conduct himself on the way to the electric chair, it seems unlikely. Starkweather's warning seems more like the cynical approximation/appropriation of a classic confession as a literary phenomena. Starkweather's statements would seem to confirm nothing less than his continued re-enforcement of his abject state as the teenage outsider.

Undoubtedly what created Reinhardt's impression that Starkweather was never truly remorseful was Starkweather's peculiar fascination with death, or rather Death, who – it would emerge in their sessions – Starkweather perceived as a female figure who would appear to him in his dreams (and, he would later claim, in the phantasmagoria of the bleary early morning). Death was – Starkweather told Reinhardt – always near him: "I knowed Death was coming".

Starkweather, according to Reinhardt, had a relationship with Death, and, in one telling quote from Starkweather, this relationship is made explicit: "Eleven people dead who wasn't expecting her and me here waiting". Starkweather had claimed that Death appeared to him not only in his dreams, but that "She comed when I was awake, too." He would wake up just before dawn and see her standing at his window: "...all I could see would be the part from the waist up. It was a kind of half human and half bear... only it didn't have no neck. It just tapered off from a big chest to a small pointed head... it didn't have no arms and no ears."

What is remarkable is that if, as Reinhardt wrote, Charles Starkweather "believed" in this closeness with/to a weird anthropomorphic feminisation of Death then why did Reinhardt – and the psychiatric community he represented – so willingly let Starkweather be found 'sane'?

At her trial, for being an accomplice to the killing of Robert Jensen, Caril Ann Fugate's lawyer, John McArthur, defended her as an innocent hostage who was forced by Starkweather to accompany him on the murderous trip. Part of the hostage defence was built around Caril's statement made during her interrogation by Chief Deputy Dale Farnbruch that she had been anally penetrated by Starkweather in the course of their sex life, an act which could be regarded as a form of abuse, and thus as an example of Starkweather's disregard for her. However the Jury, which was composed of seven men and five women, did not believe Caril's defence for several reasons. The first was as a result of Starkweather's declaration that he did not undertake the mutilations of Carol King, Mrs. Ward and Lillian Fencl, as well as the testimony against his former lover which accused Caril of the killing of Carol King. Further, although it could never be proven that Caril committed these mutilations, or was a willing accomplice with her lover, during her testimony Fugate contradicted her earlier statements to her arresting officers. When questioned about the murders of her family Caril stated that she was not aware of the killings until after Starkweather had committed them, however at the time of her arrest she told Romer that she had witnessed "all nine murders in Nebraska" (she had not been witness to the robbery of the Crest Station and the following homicide of Robert Colvert). To have witnessed these nine killings she must have also witnessed those of her family. At his summing up prosecuting attorney Scheele concluded by stating that "even fourteen-year-old girls must realize they cannot go on eight-day murder sprees." Like Charles, Carol had been 'tried' for all of the murders. On November 20th, 1958, Caril was found guilty of murder.

At only fourteen Caril was too young to be condemned to death, and was instead sentenced to life imprisonment. Caril still proclaimed her innocence as she was tearfully led to prison to begin a life sentence at the Nebraska Centre for Women. Caril would continue to insist she was kidnapped and plead not guilty until her parole in June, 1976, when – despite protests from Lincoln residents and the relatives of several victims – she emerged from prison as a fully reformed born-again Christian.

Starkweather would receive no such leniency, no reprieve, and when he heard that Caril had been sentenced to life he was reported as saying that when he went to "fry in the electric chair, Caril should be sitting in my lap". Aware of his certain fate Charles 'Little Red' Starkweather maintained the image of the nihilistic juvenile delinquent and rebel to the end; when the Nebraskan Lions Club asked if he would donate his eyes to them after his execution Starkweather was reported to have replied, "Hell no. No one ever did anything for me"; the question of the truth of this statement, whether or not Starkweather actually said this, or whether it is merely apocryphal, must be viewed as irrelevant. Starkweather was already guilty and as good as dead, to attribute such a statement to him merely lends weight to the mythology of the denim-clad rebel.

On the 25th of June, 1959, Charles Starkweather was taken from his cell on death row to the electric chair. As he was marched to the death room he showed no visible sign of emotion, and no fear, instead he shook his father's hand, hugged his mother then – hands thrust into his pockets – he slouched towards the death chamber, a remorseless teen killer to the end.

While Starkweather walked towards the grim fate of the electric chair, outside the penitentiary a group of an estimated thirty blue denim- and leather jacket-clad teenagers hung around the high gates. While others drove around the walls at the prison perimeter; car radios blaring, beer bottles swinging from their hands. One girl later told a reporter: "Some of us knew him. Some of us wanted to be with him at the end." It seemed that 'Chuck' had finally achieved the rock'n'roll notoriety he always dreamed of.

Death, the predatory goddess who Starkweather believed was always with him, played one final card; twenty-five minutes before his execution the prison physician, who was legally required to attend the execution, died of a sudden heart attack. A second physician was thus hurriedly summoned to the prison in order to attend the execution, which transpired at its scheduled time.

The prison authorities watched as Charles was lead into the death chamber, and strapped to the chair. As the executioners pulled the straps around Starkweather he was asked if he had anything to say, any final words. The teenager replied "No". The guards stepped back from his bound form, and the executioner threw the switch which sent 2,200 volts coursing through his body. The first shock was not enough to kill Starkweather and the executioners had to pull the switch a total of three times before he was declared dead, at four minutes past midnight. Starkweather's body was claimed by his family, who buried him at Wyuka Cemetery.

12

Starkweather's life, his crimes and the fearless way in which he approached the grim certainty of his execution position the teenager as an archetypal existential outsider, as he stated at the time of his arrest "I always wanted to be a criminal, but not this big a one". Starkweather's alienation from the society around him, and his profound sense of exclusion from the world, were undoubtedly based, at least in part, in the poverty in which he lived and – more importantly – felt trapped. However it was not just poverty that led to Starkweather's alienation, Starkweather's murderous spree can not be purely read in terms of class and access to wealth. The author Elliott Leyton suggests that, in part, Starkweather was killing his way "closer to the apex, up the social hierarchy from gas station attendant to working-class family to middle-class persons..."[11]. While Starkweather was certainly aware of the inequalities of his social position his *weltanschauung* was far more than an outpouring of resentment based on his disenfranchised social position. Starkweather was killing those who had status, but other aspects of his crimes contradict this, such as the killing of the maid, Fencl, who was after all 'only' a servant of the Lincoln bourgeoisie.

Charles Starkweather was not 'just' an alienated teenager and a rebel, although these elements are central to his crimes. Starkweather was also an abject, he drew attention to the very constructed-ness of both the law, and of society, and played at its boundaries, transgressing and crossing the borders placed around his social status and social relationships. His rebellion was not merely that of a juvenile delinquent, instead it was an affirmation of his status as a total outsider. The juvenile delinquent was merely a social construction, created via the discourses of cinema and media, hence Starkweather's fascination with James Dean, the quintessential socially constructed rebel. But Starkweather's crimes and his "death deal" reveal a depth to Starkweather beyond the surface social construction of the rebellious teenager. Starkweather exploded all the social relationships around him; the bonds of friendship and family were easily severed not only did he kill his friend August Meyer but he also threatened to kill his best friend Bob Von Busch, further he annihilated the entire Bartlett family, including stabbing to death the two-year-old infant (child killing is, of course, generally regarded as the most transgressive of all criminal acts). Even his relationship with Caril Ann Fugate, which provided the initial motive for the killing spree, was not sacred and within days of his arrest he was asserting her complicity within the spectacle of their crimes. Severing every relationship, including that with Caril, forced Starkweather into a position of total exclusion, a position of total outsider-ness, placing him beyond the realms of the social into an abyss from which there could be no return, as Starkweather stated, "the world is lifeless anyhow, like the people I killed". Yet this lifeless world is not the world itself but society, and Starkweather would write about the peace he felt while hunting away from all the vestiges of civilization: "I found the beauty of the country side, in forest and woods of so many times while camping or hunting." For Starkweather nature offered a purity which was unmatched elsewhere "something like directness, and frankness, in a fascinating world away from that of non-committed civilization".

It was not only the social order that Starkweather transgressed, he did not just break the most sacred taboos (homicide and infanticide), he also possessed a nihilistic death drive and hungered for his own annihilation, as Starkweather told Reinhardt; "I wanted her [Caril] to see me go down shooting it out and knowing it was for her, for us; I guess for all this hateful world has made for us" (according to Elliot Leyton Starkweather even considered crashing the car in order to 'help death'). Starkweather annihilated himself by killing those who were close to him and thus linking himself to his crimes via an easily observable motive, and further revealed his self-destructive urge to be caught by deliberately and persistently returning to the scenes of his crimes, and not fleeing their locale with the necessary velocity (it is these elements which allow the contemporary serial killer to remain undiscovered). Such a trajectory in Starkweather's crimes must be viewed as an almost suicidal drive to be caught, it could almost be seen as banal, except for the fact that Starkweather's own death drive was also a major motivation for his crimes:

"One time I was afraid to die, I used to want to shoot up the world for no reason... I was mad at the world. Then Caril made things clear; then everything had a reason. I knowed the end was coming, but it had reason to."

Finally then, when he was executed Starkweather had achieved his ultimate aim. After having been always close to death, this final step would push the teenager into a world he believed "couldn't be as bad as this one".

NOTES

1. Starkweather cited in Rheinhardt, p.40.

2. Rheinhardt, p.39.

3. Bob Von Busch quoted in Allen, p.25.

4. It has recently been suggested that many serial killers suffered similar severe blows to their head (two recent, and notorious, examples include Jeffrey Dahmer and Fredric West) and it has been suggested that such a blow could damage the brain's frontal lobes. These lobes appear to be the area of the brain which regulate the aggressive response caused by the brain's limbic system, consequently when the frontal lobes are damaged the ability to control aggression becomes reduced. Such an injury combined with various other factors, could create, at least in part, a physiological effect which plays an important part in the 'creation' of a serial killer. While such a theory is superficially attractive it should be noted that there are as many differences between killers as similarities.

5. This view was echoed by Caril's father William Fugate who stated that his ex-wife had disapproved of Caril's relationship with Starkweather.

6. The version of events which places Starkweather as a potential necrophile was confessed by Starkweather to Police Lt. Robert Henninger. Starkweather would later deny this confession.

7. The letter was supposedly written by Starkweather and Fugate, and it switches its first person narrative from Charles to Caril almost at random, however its grammatical style implies that the letter was written by Charles alone. Note also that it implicates Caril within the crimes.

8. Anderson was also one of the last people to see C. Lauer Ward alive, the two men had just completed a meeting before Ward returned home and was killed.

9. Quoted in Associated Press, "Teenager Seized In The Slaying of 10", *The New York Times*, January 30th, 1958.

10. Starkweather was granted a stay of execution so that he could testify against Fugate. Starkweather's new date of execution was June 12th 1959, but this date too was postponed – a mere two days before it was scheduled to transpire – in order that an appeal could be made in the Supreme Court. The Supreme Court refused the petition for a hearing and Starkweather's execution date was set, once more, for June 25th, 1959. Starkweather would be the last person to be executed by the State of Nebraska.

11. Leyton, *Hunting Humans*, p.235.

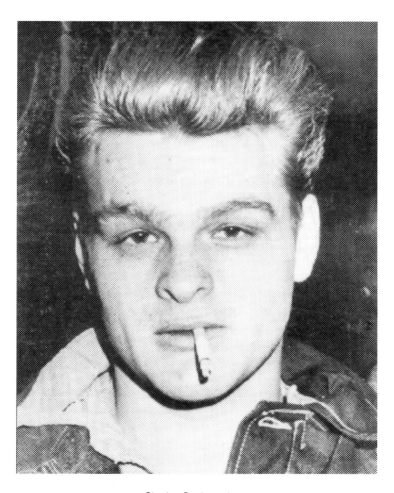

Charles Starkweather

Charles Starkweather and Caril Ann Fugate

The storm cave where Robert Jensen's body was found

Robert Jensen's body

Commotion outside the Ward residence

Two Are Held in Wyoming in a Series of Slayings

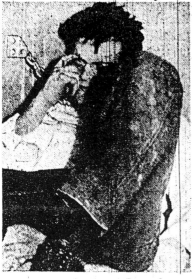

Charles Starkweather, 19, in a jail cell at Douglas, Wyo., after he was captured.

Caril Fugate, 14, at jail. She had fled with Starkweather from Lincoln, Neb.

The New York Times   Jan. 30, 1958

9 victims were found near Lincoln, Neb. (1); suspect seized at Douglas, Wyo. (2).

The *New York Times*, January 30, 1958

NEBRASKA TO TRY YOUTH AS SLAYER

DOUGLAS, Wyo., Jan. 30 (AP) —Nebraska officers won custody today of Charles Starkweather, 19-year-old garbage truck driver who police say is responsible for the slaying of eleven persons.

Starkweather and his 14-year-old girl friend, Caril Ann Fugate, signed extradition papers agreeing to return to Lincoln, Neb., where they face murder charges.

Shortly afterward the heavily guarded couple — in separate cars—were started on the 500-mile trip to Lincoln.

Wyoming, accusing Starkweather of another murder, readily yielded to Nebraska's demands for the youth, captured here yesterday. Nebraska inflicts the death penalty in an electric chair.

Starkweather has said Caril had no part in the killings. He ate heartily in his jail cell today

A matron described the Fugate girl as stunned and dazed. She ate lightly.

Nine persons were killed in Nebraska this week and another, a Montana salesman, near Douglas yesterday. A detective said he thought Starkweather was involved in the slaying of a Lincoln filling station operator, Robert Colvert, 21, Dec. 1.

The *New York Times*, January 31, 1958

MURDER IS DENIED

Starkweather Enters Plea to One of Eleven Charges

LINCOLN, Neb., Feb. 3 (UP)
—Charles Starkweather pleaded
not guilty today to charges of
murdering one of eleven persons
he earlier confessed to killing.

County Attorney Elmer Scheele said the confession told in
detail how the 19-year-old
Starkweather, aided by Caril
Fugate, 14, killed Robert Jensen, 17, and Carol King, 16, of
Bennet, Neb., a week ago today.

Starkweather was arraigned
on charges of first degree murder. The charges referred to the
Jensen killing only, although
Starkweather and Caril have
also been charged with the slaying of Miss King.

Caril later entered a not
guilty plea to similar charges
in the Jensen killing.

The girl has insisted she was
Starkweather's unwilling hostage during the two-state rampage. Starkweather has asserted
she was his willing accomplice.

The *New York Times*, February 4, 1958

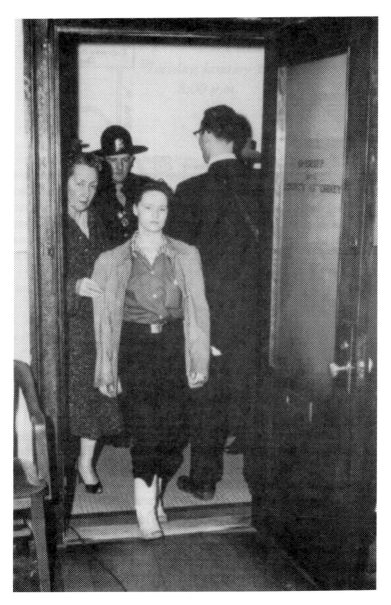

Caril Fugate in custody

Starkweather in prison after his arrest

Starkweather enters the State Penitentiary, May 24 1958,
minutes after being sentenced to death

Self-portrait by Charles Starkweather

Drawing by Charles Starkweather

Drawing by Charles Starkweather

"Rebellion"

started pounding hard against my breast, and I began to weaken in moral strength; for the love of my dear Mom, Dad, my Sister and Brothers, I always thought I could conquer the world that I hated, with-out any help from home, or from the family, but I was very, - very, - wrong, the affection for my family is as ardent, and strong, as the love for our Jesus Christ. I thought of the nice Sunday picnics, and of many other happy times we all had together. They,

Page from *Rebellion*

"Rebellion"

raised in this house through most
of my child-hood, the place to me
looked like a enchanted forest, with
its large trees surrounding the
house, and at times in the evening
when the sun was setting in its
tender glory, with it's beautiful
colors in the western sky, and
the birds singing in their melodys
that came softly from the trees, —
everything was nice and pretty,
so peaceful, and tranquil, — it was
as though time it self was standing

Page from *Rebellion*

still. I fell in love with this "Rebellion"
adventurous land in my earlier
days, and the flame still burns
deep down inside of me for the love
of that enchanted forest.

The house was a shabby white
one story structure with five
Bed-rooms, a Living, and Dining-
room, a Kitchen, with a pantry,
six Closets, and full size Bath-rooms.
also there was a full size Basement,
which had a build in store room
at one corner. The front porch

Page from *Rebellion*

Death certificate of Charles Starkweather

Role model: James Dean, *Rebel Without A Cause*

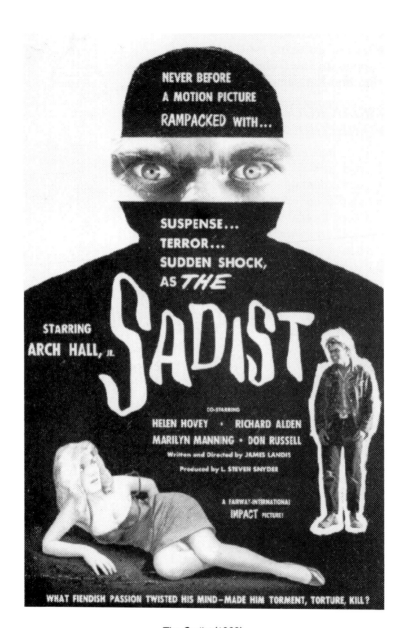

The Sadist (1963)

Badlands (1974)

Badlands (1974)

Badlands (1974)

Badlands (1974)

Badlands (1974)

Wild At Heart (1990)

True Romance (1993)

Kalifornia (1993)

Kalifornia (1993)

Natural Born Killers (1994)

Natural Born Killers (1994)

Natural Born Killers (1994)

Gun Crazy
Starkweather and Fugate on Film:
Notes towards a Cinematic Sub-Genre

The Charles Starkweather and Caril Ann Fugate story has formed the basis for a series of films, spanning three decades of both mainstream – which is the focus of this paper – and marginal cinema[1]. This paper seeks to examine the most clearly analogous films to the Starkweather/Fugate story, and it is not intended to be either a definitive or complete history of this sub-genre.[2]

The concept of film genre, it could be argued, is manifested in two distinct forms, either as a cinematic mode of production or as a theoretical construction designed for the benefit of critical exploration and/or analysis. The first of these forms of genre – that of genre as a mode of production – emerges from an economic and ideological interpretation of Hollywood's film output. This form of cinematic genre describes the way in which film production could be regulated via a standardization of filmmaking practices, and the repetition across a series of cinematic texts of a recognizable narrative form, iconography and *mise-en-scène*. Such a standardization enables both the film industry and the audience to engage with the cinematic text through a series of expectations about the movie. The second manifestation of genre – that of genre as a theoretical construction – retrospectively imagines a genre in order to examine a group of film texts. The primary example of this distinction would be Film Noir, a recognized genre which was constructed retrospectively in order to examine a collection of disparate texts (such as Thrillers, gangster movies, Melodramas). The genre this essay examines is constructed across more than

---

twenty years of film production, and is, primarily, a sub-genre of the Road Movie, but bears the important distinction of being influenced by Starkweather and Fugate's nihilistic and murderous distortion of the on-the-road teenage romance.

The inaugural gesture, or at least the most clearly apparent articulation, of this sub-genre is in Terrence Malick's *Badlands* (1974)[3]. The film – despite its textual protestations to being a work of fiction – is an almost exact recreation of Starkweather and Fugate's relationship, although it is not without its noticeable differences. Nevertheless it is to this film that other works within the sub-genre refer; it is *Badlands* – rather than Starkweather's actual story – which serves as the general point of intertextuality throughout this sub-genre (although each film has many other points of intertextuality which are culturally and temporally specific to that text and its particular audience). As *Badlands* maintains such a central position in this sub-genre it is worth examining in some depth before moving on to other texts within the cannon.

Badlands depicts the relationship between the twenty-five-year-old Kit Crothers (Martin Sheen) and the fifteen-year-old androgen Holly (Sissy Spacek), the film is narrated by Holly who describes her family background and her move from Texas to the small town of Fort Dupret, South Dakota, with her father, following the death of her mother. The film opens with Holly's narration and simultaneously we see the garbage truck and garbage men; Kit and Cato, Kit is sorting through the trash when he comes across a dead dog, meanwhile Holly's flat – almost naively lifeless – narration intones: "Little did I realize that what began in the alleys and backstreets of this small town would end in the badlands of Montana". Kit and Holly meet one afternoon while she plays in the street and he walks home from his garbage route, and the two begin talking. While the two get on Holly immediately articulates her father's displeasure at the idea of her dating a garbage man, but confesses her own desire "he was handsomer than anyone I'd ever met, he looked just like James Dean". Shortly after this Kit loses his job as a garbage

Born Bad

man and becomes a cowboy, all the while Holly's narration describes the growth of their relationship.

Unfortunately Holly's father finds out about their relationship, and forbids the two from seeing each other. Kit goes to speak to Holly's father, Holly, says Kit "means an awful lot to me". Holly's father is unimpressed by Kit's declarations of love for his daughter, and Kit leaves. Kit later enters Holly's house and packs her bags for her, as he completes the task Holly's father walks in, and demands to know what is happening, Kit produces a gun, Holly's father threatens to tell the authorities and Kit shoots him in the stomach. Holly is obviously upset and thinks they should tell the authorities, to which the cooly nihilistic Kit replies "if you wanna tell the police that's fine, but it wouldn't be so hot for me". Holly, who until the end of the narrative lets others make her decisions (her narration states at one stage that she has no personality), decides against telling the authorities, and Kit goes into town to make a record stating that he and Holly are going to kill themselves. He then dowses the house in petrol and sets it on fire, while a record player positioned in the garden plays the suicide note/record. Holly picks up her school books and her narration states "my destiny now lay with Kit".

Kit and Holly (who are now, according to the narration, suitably renamed, presumably after their chosen idols; James [Dean] and Priscilla [Presley]) initially hide out in the woods, building a Tarzan style tree house above a small clearing, which Kit fills with suitably Vietnam style booby traps. They are soon discovered and Kit – hiding in a branch-covered pit – ambushes the three law men presumably sent to investigate, killing them all. The two lovers then hit the road, first stopping off at Cato's lonely house. Here they eat a meal before walking out into the surrounding fields, while Kit and Holly walk ahead Cato turns and flees, heading towards his small house. Kit raises his gun and shoots Cato in the back. They take Cato back to his house, where he slowly bleeds to death. Soon afterwards two teenagers drive up to visit Cato, and when they refuse to offer a lift to Kit and Holly, Kit takes them out to an abandoned cellar, locks them in the cramped space and fires a volley of shots through the trap door, presumably killing the young couple. Holly's voice over: "Kit was the most trigger happy person I'd ever met".

Kit and Holly drive to a wealthy area of town, here they knock on the door of a large house, which is opened by a deaf maid. Kit and Holly hold the maid and her male employer hostage. While at the house a friend-cum-business associate calls at the house (a brief cameo by Malick), but Kit sends him away warning that everybody has flu. Kit and Holly then lock up the maid and the rich man, as they do this Kit hands the rich man a list of everything that they have 'borrowed' (taken from the house). The two lovers then leave the house and hit the road, driving out across the great plains, following the telephone lines heading towards the distant quasi-mythological mountains of Montana. Eventually – low on fuel – they stop by an oil derrick, but before they can re-fuel a helicopter spots them. To Kit's dismay Holly elects to stay behind, essentially surrendering to the forces of law and order. Kit is pursued across the badlands by a passing police car, Kit engages in a high speed chase before eventually stopping his car, building a small stack of stones as a memorial to where he was caught, and – as the pursuing police car screeches to a halt – surrendering. Finally – awaiting to be returned home to face his trial – Kit stands chained, amiably talking to the police and National Guardsmen and obviously enjoying playing the role of the murderous celebrity. Through the narration we learn that Kit dies in the electric chair, while Holly gets off on parole and eventually marries her lawyer's son.

Badlands presents Kit and Holly fleeing the 'real' world and emerging themselves in the fantasy of their own world. Everything in their life has a bland boredom to it, as if they are children who are perpetually dissatisfied but lack even the energy to articulate this frustration. The one attempt at sex presented in the film ends in a blank orgasmless un-climax, followed by a brief conversation (no conversation they have in the film appears to go beyond the most superficial exchange of rudimentary information). The murders themselves (other than Holly's very brief show of emotion at her fathers death) are greeted with a similar lack of emotion, Kit 'just' shoots people and Holly watches, appearing as an emotionless androgen in contrast to Kit's almost silent nihilism. Kit's nihilism, is however, a lifeless deadening nihilism which marks Kit as its victim rather than its avatar, and ultimately Kit is seduced by the mimesis of nihilistic cool rather than actual nihilism.

The world which Kit and Holly invent for themselves is a simulation of domestic bliss, this becomes most apparent in the sequence set in the woods, during which the film presents them living as an almost archetypal married couple, the only thing which separates them from the 'real' world being Kit's crimes and the intensity of the emotional void in which they live.

What is seen of the relationship between the protagonists – primarily Holly – and the 'real' world is underlined with a spectacular violence. Kit is obviously an outcast, even among his work mates at the garbage department and, later, the ranch, and he is often presented as distanced from other people. More importantly, however, is the depiction of Holly's relationship with her father, a relationship which is characterized by an extremity of violence and abuse, thus, for example, when Holly begins dating Kit and her father finds out he takes her puppy into a field and shoots it.

Badlands is hauntingly scored – to great effect – with music by Carl Orff and Eric Satie, which creates an almost hypnagogic effect. Such an effect is further emphasized via the deadpan, listless, narration which, for the most part, describes the day to day mundanity of the relationship, rather than Holly's actual emotions or relationship with Kit. During one key sequence, while the lovers are staying at the mansion, Holly goes out for a short walk around its grounds and, in a rarely incisive moment, describes her feeling of exclusion from the world, and as being like an outsider looking in at the 'normal world'. The journey she has taken with Kit is thus marked as more than just physical but also as psychic, a journey which has taken them from the realm of the social into their own special world. The dream-like quality evoked by the soundtrack adds to this feeling of outsiderness, an effect which is most emphasized by the film's *mise-en-scène*.

Badlands' cinematography similarly serves to emphasize the couple's outsider status, a status characterised by the disappearance of the traditionally ascribed borders. While the narrative focuses on the transgression of the rule of law, and entry into a zone of wilful exclusion, of outsiderness, the *mise-en-scène* reiterates this narrative trajectory of the boundary transgressing and borderless state. This is most apparent in the scenes set in the badlands, here the great plains are shot as an almost hellish infinity of flat, empty miles, mirrored by the flatness of the sky above them. Only Kit and Holly's car breaks the endless monotony of the landscape. The geography is filmed to emphasise its 'collapse', until the horizon seems to vanish into pure flatness; world and sky as one massive blank canvas. Such a landscape can only ever be identified as borderless; as infinite; the collapse of distinction between sky and earth merely reiterating the collapse of all other borders and boundaries within the narrative. As the French postmodern theorist Jean Baudrillard wrote, when describing the interminable flatness of the American deserts:

"You are delivered from all depth there – a brilliant, mobile, superficial neutrality, a challenge to meaning and profundity, a challenge to nature and culture, an outer hyperspace, with no origin, no reference-points"[4].

Except for the teleological ramifications of eschatology and eschatological thinking, which render it as mere metaphysical construction, it would almost be possible to describe the appearance of this flat, endless landscape as apocalyptic (such end-time geographic eschatology becoming far more apparent in the other texts mentioned below).

Badlands also introduces, and plays with, a series of signifier which serve to emphasize, and to punctuate, the nature of Kit and Holly's relationship. The most apparent of these is the image of the fire which burns down Holly's family home. This consuming fire is filmed so as to emphasize the flames as they annihilate the very heart of 'traditionally ascribed values' and of order – the family home. The fire serves to delineate the change between 'normal'/'perverse', between 'family values'/ 'amorality', and between 'innocence'/'guilt'. Not only does the fire mark a narrative point of no return, it also marks a psychic point of no return, a zenith from which the characters emerge as 'changed', or – rather – 'changing', like the distant mountains the characters never reach, so a state of 'being' never emerges in their journey, instead the two lovers exist in a state of continually negated being, a theme which will be more fully explored below.

Another element introduced by *Badlands* is that of the personalized ritual of affirmation. These rituals are personalized versions of the marriage ceremony, in *Badlands* there are two major ritualised moments (excluding the burning of the house, which may also be interpreted as a version of a ritual of abandoning childhood). The first ritual is the making of a balloon which Kit and Holly fill with various totems and tokens of their love for each other before sending it floating above the fields on the outskirts of town. The second ritual in the film – performed by Kit and Holly shortly before their separation and Kit's final chase and capture – repeats this, but reverses the gesture, instead of sending the effects spiralling skyward the two lovers bury a bucket of tokens in the desert (this difference demarking the different state of their relationship, which rather than affirming becomes a thing to be buried and hidden). There are other rituals in the film, although they are less about the couple's relationship than about Kit, for example after their first fuck Kit wants to mark the spot with a stone, and at the film's climax – shortly before Kit is apprehended – he marks the spot with a small stack of stones.

The most obvious – yet perhaps the most crucial – signifier *Badlands* plays with is that of the couple's relationship to the car. The car represents far more than 'only' their mode of transport; it represents both the (relative) stability of Kit and Holly's home (primarily when they have to flee into the *Badlands*) and the very key to their achieving their fantasies and desires. At night they can dance in the glare of its headlights, while listening to the music coming from its radio, on a more general level the car itself is also a central element in the mythology of American culture, and specifically youth culture, and the car must be seen as a part of teenage culture which, at least in the '50s, was equal to rock'n'roll in its ability to demark a territory of difference from previous generations. The car is what enables them to commit their crimes and escape, it offers them transport and shelter while they drive towards the distant Montana mountains which provide them (although ultimately only Kit, as Holly becomes aware of the flaws in the fantasy) with their hope, their 'Emerald City'.

Following *Badlands* the next major film to engage with the Starkweather and Fugate influenced thematic of pursued love was David Lynch's *Wild At Heart*. While the film is neither a direct reference to the Starkweather and Fugate story – as *Badlands* surely was – nor thematically a pure teenage-killers-on-the-road narrative, the film does contain many elements in common with both the sub-genre's thematics and with its attendant iconography.

Wild At Heart focuses on the relationship between Sailor Ripley (Nicholas Cage) and Lula (Laura Dern). Sailor, having just served a prison sentence for manslaughter (defending himself from a killer sent by Lula's mother), flees Cape Fear with his lover Lula. However Lula's mother – a mimesis of the Wicked Witch from *The Wizard Of Oz*, the quintessential road film – asks small time gangster Santos to intervene in the romance and kill Sailor.

Fleeing the evil of Lola's mother, Sailor and Lula drive from Cape Fear to New Orleans, and finally to Big Tuna, Texas ("It ain't exactly Emerald City" deadpans Sailor). The town is populated by Lynch's regular cast of oddballs, misfits and freaks, and from this point onwards the film 'drops' its love-on-the-run thematic, replacing it with the narrative of a small town heist. Once settled in Big Tuna, Sailor is manipulated, by contract killers working for Santos, into participating in a robbery which transpires in the nearby town of Lobo. Sailor is not aware that, during the robbery, he will be 'accidentally' shot. Luckily for Sailor the robbery is interrupted by the police before he is murdered, and consequently he survives the heist-cum-bloodbath, and – after spending six years in prison – he is re-united with Lula and their six-year-old son, Pace.

Wild At Heart is a postmodern text, and as such it embraces a series of aesthetic strategies; generic deconstruction, pastiche, and intertextuality. The film thus offers a repeated series of references (stylistic, visual and textual) primarily to *The Wizard Of Oz*, as well as to *Badlands*, Jean Luc Godard's *Weekend* and Nicholas Ray's *Johnny Guitar*, as well as non-cinematic manifestations of popular culture, primarily via the text's repeated references to Elvis Presley.

Wild At Heart uses many signifier introduced by *Badlands*, such a repetition marks *Wild At Heart*'s postmodern bricolage, however it must also be read as a specifically generic reference. The first of these elements is once again that of geography. While *Wild At Heart* focuses on the geography of the American South and Texas, rather than the great plains of the Midwest, it still utilises a geography which emphasizes the breakdown of the borders created by law and order. Rather than emphasising the vast inescapable flatness of the geography *Wild At Heart* uses the endless-ness of the wind torn desert, a land which so over invested in symbolic meaning in the texts of the Western's that, now as barren as the dreams it once nurtured, has come to mean nothing except the very lack of certainty in any hope or dream. This is emphasised by the pathetically named Big Tuna, Texas, a nearly deserted town which appears totally landlocked in the middle of a dustbowl. Further the Texan desert, a land rich in oil, becomes a site of a spectacularly grotesque car crash, as Sailor and Lula come across a bloodied teenager, stumbling around a wrecked car, searching for her money and her purse, two signifiers of identity and certainty, which remain unfound as the injured teenager gurgles and vomits to her grave. The desert landscape becomes thus associated directly with a loss of all boundaries of self and identity, and becomes immediately associated with an apocalyptic return to chaos[5].

Like *Badlands*, *Wild At Heart* also plays with the image of fire as an image of change. *Wild At Heart* continually replays the fire image via extreme close-ups of matches/cigarettes as well as the image of a flaming house. Like *Badlands* the fire in *Wild At Heart* is the signifier for change, although the fire has already occurred in the narrative of *Wild At Heart* via flash backs within the narrative the audience learn that this fire is responsible for the death of Lula's father, and consequently the pursuit of the two lovers, because Sailor was the driver for the villainous Santos who actually set the fire. The fire is thus the event which is responsible for the current predicament of the fugitive lovers, just as it was in *Badlands*, the only difference being that *Wild At Heart* is also playing with the *noir* genre and is consequently using the gangsters who started the fire as the reason for the lovers fleeing, rather than blaming the fire on the lovers themselves. Further the fire in *Wild At Heart* was in part started for the benefit of Lula's mother, a mother who is characterised via a sadistic violence which is manifested via a desire to dominate Lula's sexuality and desires via the destruction of her relationship with Sailor, once again echoing the destructive father in *Badlands*.

Wild At Heart places less emphasis on specific rituals demarking the relationship (which is unusual in this sub-genre, see below), however its emphasis on the sexuality of Sailor Ripley and Lula, and the narratives repeated emphasis on their post-coital conversations, serves to emphasize the strength of their relationship. Sailor also repeatedly describes his snakeskin jacket as a symptom of his individuality, and the jacket becomes a symbol of exchange between Sailor and Lula at several points in the narrative, and thus may also be said to mark a ritual. The most significant ritual that the film introduces, however, is that of the couple's relationship to dancing, both elements which feature only at the margins of the text in *Badlands* become central in *Wild At Heart*. Dancing in *Wild At Heart* becomes an act which signifies the separation of Lula and Sailor from the rest of the society around them; initially Lynch presents Sailor and Lula at a heavy metal concert, dancing together but apart; they do not touch each other, but as soon as somebody 'bumps into' Lula they stop dancing and Sailor confronts the man. Sailor then serenades Lula with an Elvis song, drawing a direct link between the archetypal '50s rebel and his own – often stated – individuality. Later in the film Lynch depicts Lula driving the car, however – unable to find any dance music on the radio – she screams and slams the brakes on. Running from the car she demands that Sailor find a channel playing dance music. He flips the dial, until he finds a station blaring heavy metal, then leaps out of the car and the two dance together, but still not touching but just kicking and leaping through the air. Yet as the song ends and they stop dancing they come together and embrace at the roadside in the light of the setting sun. While there is a deliberate engagement with the questions of pastiche and cinema in Lynch's text the film nevertheless fits into the sub-genre, through its use of the same thematics and iconographic signifiers.

Like *Wild At Heart*, Tony Scott's *True Romance*, 1993, (based on the first script by Hollywood's current *wunderkind* Quentin Tarantino) plays with the thematic of pursued love, and cinematic references to *Badlands* without actually being a direct teen killers on the run movie. The film builds a thriller/crime narrative around the young lovers' romance. *True Romance* opens in Detroit, and follows a twenty-something comic book shop employee, film buff and loner, Clarence, as he meets and fall in love with call girl, Alabama. Within twenty four hours the two young lovers are married, and Alabama sports a tattoo bearing the legend 'Clarence' on her midriff.

Clarence is upset when Alabama tells him of the abuse she suffered at the hands of her sleazy pimp Drexyl, and – after taking advice from Elvis Presley who appears to Clarence while the newly wed is taking a piss – Clarence vows 'vengeance'. Telling Alabama not to worry Clarence takes a pistol and, after receiving a beating from Drexyl and his thug associate, Clarence kills them. Telling another hooker to give him Alabama's belongings Clarence returns to his apartment. (Un)fortunately instead of getting Alabama's clothes Clarence has picked up a suitcase full of uncut coke. The two lovers decide to travel across country to Los Angeles to sell the coke and spend the rest of their lives having fun on the profits, before they leave town they go and say goodbye to Clarence's father. Unfortunately for Clarence and Alabama the coke was not just Drexyl's but belongs to Sicilian gangster Blue Lou, who sends crazed henchman Vincenzo to torture Clarence's father and find out where the two lovers have gone.

In Los Angeles, Clarence and Alabama meet up with Clarence's old friend Dick and his stoned flatmate Floyd. Dick agrees to introduce Clarence to various movie makers, gradually leading up the hierarchy to a director called Lee. Before a meeting can be set up Alabama is attacked by one of Blue Lou's associates, who viciously beats her before she can kill him. Meanwhile creepy Hollywood drug connection Elliot, who will introduce the couple to Lee, is busted by the police. By the time the two lovers get to meet Lee, Elliot has been wired by the LAPD and the gangsters are on the way. In the ensuing shoot-out everybody (Hollywood drug dealers, directors, cops and Blue Lou's henchmen) is killed except for Clarence, Alabama and Dick. Dick flees mid-shoot out to appear in an episode of *TJ Hooker*, while Clarence and Alabama take the money and move to Mexico.

Along with *Wild At Heart*, *True Romance* plays with the iconography of Elvis Presley, who appears twice in the film to advise Clarence, acting as a symbol of rebellion but also as a paternal figure; a fantasy father. Elvis acts as a signifier for an archetypical American youthful rebellion, and simultaneously offers a camp humour in the film, as well as offering a point of intertextuality with films such as *Wild At Heart* and Jim Jarmusch's *Mystery Train*. *True Romance* also makes repeated references to *Badlands* via its main theme, which is a virtual re-working of the *Badlands* soundtrack. Further *True Romance* utilises an opening and closing narration from Alabama (who, like Holly, has a southern accent, a theme addressed below). This narration describes the nature of true romance, and the fleeting possibilities it offers and the particular violent insanity that this romance inspired. The narration's only difference from Holly's narration is that it acts as a pure affirmation to the relationship at both the opening and close of the text.

What is remarkable about *True Romance* is that, despite being about love on the run, the central protagonists actually spend very little time on the road, at least as it is generally viewed in Road Movies. Instead the journey across the country is reduced to the bare minimum, but Los Angeles, rather than representing the utopia at the journey's end (as it would come to mean in *Kalifornia*) becomes a zone identified with the journey. Thus, rather than being constructed as a city by the text, Los Angeles becomes identified with the road, as Clarence and Alabama cruise in their pink Cadillac from location to location in order to set up the coke deal. Jean Baudrillard suggests that Los Angeles itself is a zone of freeways which render the city as "an inhabited fragment of the desert"[6] The only place of relative stasis, the only geographically fixed 'home', is the motel room at which the couple stay, and this space can only operate as a temporary space, with the narrative function of allowing the couple to store the drugs, and as the place where Alabama is attacked. Even the 'native' residents of the city are always presented as in transit; thus Elliot is busted by the police while driving. For Elliot the car is not just the place where he 'gets high' but also the place where he makes his phone calls from, and receives blow jobs from dumb starlets, all while driving along the Pacific Coast Highway at high speed. Similarly Dick's apartment is a place characters always either arrive at or leave but never stay at. The only person to remain at the apartment is Floyd, who never appears to leave it, but just sits watching television while continually smoking copious quantities of marijuana and – blissfully unaware – telling collective gangsters about Clarence's dealings; to be still is thus identified with a psychic stasis as much as a physical stasis. By emphasising the city itself as a place of perpetual motion *True Romance* emphasizes the continued velocity of Clarence and Alabama's journey without ever actually emphasizing a 'going to' (save for the coda at the film's end), instead their destination – rather than physical – becomes the achievement of their desire to make money with the coke deal. Desire is thus transformed from the physical locale of an actual utopia (such as *Badlands'* Montana mountains, or *Kalifornia* in California) to the psychic zone.

Dominic Sena's 1993 film *Kalifornia* also engages with a re-working of *Badlands* and the Starkweather/Fugate narrative, although – unlike *Wild At Heart* – the film does not engage with a generic bricolage, but rather returns to the original format, but extends it via the introduction of a second couple of young lovers. *Kalifornia* (the replacement of the 'C' with the 'K' acting as a signifier of the films thanatopic thematic; Kali – at least in one of her forms, and certainly that most favoured by the generally ethnocentric metanarrative of Hollywood cinema – is the goddess of chaos and destruction) depicts two couples as they drive from the East coast to the West coast of America. One couple, Brian Kestler and Carrie, are identified as being middle-class, educated and northern. Brian – who offers both an extra-diagetic and internal narration throughout the film – is a writer who, armed with his dictaphone, is travelling to sites of famous murders and recording his observations and the particular criminal and personal histories which have led to such crimes. Offered the chance of writing his first book, Brian decides to drive across America to California via these grim locales. In order to fully document this journey Brian asks his partner, Carrie, to accompany him. Carrie is an art photographer (this is made apparent by the film's depiction of her repeated rejection at galleries for being too obscure, in fact her pictures appear as stark chiaroscuro erotica, most of which appear to depict carefully posed pictures of black men and white women) who agrees to travel across the country taking photographs of the murder sites which Brian is writing about. The ultimate aim is to produce the book, but – more importantly – it is to reach California, "a place of hopes and dreams" Brian's narration states. In California he will be a writer and Carrie a photographer, for the couple it represents the land of limitless opportunity.

In order to finance the trip Brian and Carrie decide to place an advertisement in the nearby university in order to split the cost of gasoline (noticeably the sign placed on the notice board by Brian reads 'Kalifornia'). The sign is immediately picked up by the school janitor (of one day), Early Grace. Early has been sent to the university by his parole officer, a disgusting figure who makes it clear that he feels the derogatory position is more than suitable for the recently paroled Early.

Early lives in a trailer, which is parked in a run down garbage heap, with his girlfriend Adele (who, as the film progresses, the audience learn has been the victim of an exceptionally violent rape at some point in her past). Early decides to jump parole and head with Adele for California, a land he believes has fruit on every tree which is just waiting to be picked, additionally – he tells Adele – "the first month rent is free". Early kills his scumbag landlord, sets fire to the trailer and, with Adele, joins Brian and Carrie on the journey west, the pair unaware that one of their passengers is a homicidal maniac (like *Badlands'* Kit, Early's murderous intensities are linked to 'insanity'; while Kit has visions while in the early morning hypnogia between sleep and wakefulness, Early believes in doors which are geo-temporal gateways between dimensions, each offering a new potentiality. It should also be noted that Brian's narration fixes the serial killer as inhabiting a psychic state which is "between dreams and reality").

The two couples are antithetical, while Carrie and Brian are bourgeois liberal artists Early and Adele are described as "Oakies" and "white trash". Against the designer black denim of the artists Early and Adele dress in ultra-downbeat thrift store trash; he in faded Hawaian shirt, she in boob tubes and halter top. More importantly the difference is marked by Early's baseball cap which bares the Confederate cross, and the accents of the 'white trash' which are unmistakably Southern. It is thus not merely psychology, profession or class which divide the two couples so much as the Macon Dixie Line. Since the American Civil War the South has been identified with exceptional poverty, and the profound loss of cultural identity. This is, in part, due to both the loss of its separate identity (which was supported by a romantic myth of social harmony), via the ending of slavery and hence its wealth, but also as a result of the North's cultural imperialism.

As the journey progresses so Early funds his petrol contributions by murdering and stealing. Meanwhile Carrie becomes increasingly concerned; first becoming aware that Early has been in prison, then that he beats Adele and finally that he has a gun. While Carrie becomes worried, Brian is seduced by the potential violence inaugurated by Early; firstly when – on a drunken night out – he witnesses Early's prowess in a bar-room brawl, and later when Early lets him fire his gun. Eventually, at a deserted garage in the middle of the desert, Carrie sees a television news program which shows footage of Early before stating that he is wanted for questioning on various murder charges after having jumped bail. Early then shows his true colours and takes over, holding Brian and Carrie hostage as he drives them all to California, killing everybody who gets in the way.

In a noticeable reference to *Badlands*, Early pulls the car into the drive of a large house owned by an evidently wealthy elderly couple. In the house Early ties up Brian and Carrie, and kills the elderly male resident, while the elderly female flees into the desert night. Like the house in *Badlands* (and the Ward residence in the Starkweather/Fugate case) the house in

Kalifornia is a signifier of the wealthy world from which Early and Adele are permanently excluded. Similarly Early and Adele are seduced by the house, exploring it and relishing its opulence (this is primarily true of Adele who marvels at the collection of cacti which sit throughout – and in pots outside – the house). Like Holly in *Badlands*, Adele is marked by her own apparent lack of personality and is frequently ignored by the protagonists (during one early sequence Adele comments on the need of communication and friends in the development of a personality, while she speaks everybody ignores her), while at the house Adele realises – finally – that Early is a scum bag, and she articulates this before clubbing him with a cactus. His response is to kill her.

Having killed Adele, Early beats Brian senseless and kidnaps Carrie. He then takes Carrie to California, but decides to spend the night in Nevada, hiding out in a simulated town, which is actually an old nuclear test site. Here he rapes Carrie, although not before she stabs him. At dawn the following day Brian arrives, as the sun rises over the nuclear landscape he fights and kills Early. The film cuts, and the audience witnesses Brian and Carrie living in California, his book is nearly finished, and Carrie has had interest from a gallery in showing her work.

Kalifornia utilises the generic iconography, although various iconographic elements are re-worked by being either updated or used with a different emphasis. The image of fire does not directly occur in *Kalifornia*, instead Early's initial killing (which transpires at the film's opening) takes place in torrential rain, thus the chaos and destruction of fire is mirrored by the chaos and destruction of water, the elemental status of the signifier is still relevant to the narrative. When Early 'reveals' his murderous nature it is at a deserted garage during the middle of a massive electrical storm, and the scene is repeatedly marked with images of lightning and wind. The storm is elemental, threatening and marking change in much a similar way as fire in *Badlands* and *Wild At Heart*.

The film also depicts contrary rituals of affirmation between the two couples; while Carrie and Brian engage in mutual discussions of art or career, Early and Adele repeatedly slide into the zone of their own language, singing childlike sexual (yet simultaneously naive) songs to each other. In a reversal of the affirmation offered by music and dancing, *Kalifornia* depicts music and dancing as an escape from the killer couple's relationship; when Adele is told by Carrie that Early is a murderer, Adele turns the car radio onto full volume and begins to dance. Music thus acts as an anaesthetic for Adele rather than a signifier of her closeness to Early.

Kalifornia offers an update of the apocalyptic geography which signifies the boundary transgressions of the genre's murderous protagonists. The landscape goes 'beyond' the desert to the post-nuclear (literal) apocalyptic test site town. While the family background of Early and Adele remains under suspension[7] throughout the text (during one hilarious sequence Brian tries to stop Early killing a wounded policeman, "look, he's not your father" Brian states. "I know that" says Early, as if Brian is stating the obvious, then casually blasts the cop to death). The abandoned desert town reiterates the violence which could be said to be characteristic of 'normal' daily life. Standing in the living room of the test site house is the archetypal 'nuclear' family (pun clearly intended) made from mannequins. *Kalifornia* thus expressly makes the connection between the (plastic) post-war family and the mindless rampage of the serial killer, all of whom are linked with the 'terror' of the family home, a place which mirrors the hellish violence of the apocalyptic world beyond the four walls of the house. A world which is clearly signified by the radioactive desert, but is also present throughout the whole film in the abandoned and decrepit industrial wastelands through which the group drives. This apocalyptic theme is further iterated via the rant of a wino seen in the diner where Adele works. The wino sits in the diner talking (to nobody) about the Biblical apocalypse. Various other supporting characters also have a quasi-apocalyptic appearance, looking as if they have been visited by some grotesque plague, for example: Early's parole officer has a violent hacking cough and is missing a hand, Early and Adele's landlord is obesely overweight and is surrounded by a small pack of ugly copulating dogs, finally a victim who is slaughtered in the toilet of a gas station is seen releasing the contents of a catheter bag into the urinal due – presumably – to some urinary disfunction.

By the introduction of the second couple (Brian and Carrie) *Kalifornia* both explores, and problematizes, the narrative structure. Firstly via the second couple the film allows the audience to engage with a series of complex multiple identifications, which reflect back and forth across couples and genders, this is far more clearly apparent than in *Badlands*, where the audience is never able to fully identify, nor disavow an identification, with the killer couple. *Badlands'* flatness – and the repeated re-emphasis of this flatness – serves to distance the audience from any identification. *Kalifornia*, with its traditional shot/reverse-shot style and established generic narrative, allows for what could be considered (at least 'traditionally') to be a more ready mode of identification but by switching the audiences possible identifications across four characters throughout the text serves to create a potentially liberating schizophrenia.

Brian and Carrie also serve to emphasize the audience's own ambiguous relationship to the text: the cinematic audience's voyeurism and scopophilia is mirrored by that of Brian and Carrie who are repeatedly depicted acting out their/the audience's thanatopic fascination. Thus the audience witness violence in parallel to the violence which Brian and Carrie's project fetishizes, this reaches its zenith when, in an abandoned slaughterhouse, Brian plays a cassette of a girl begging for her life while being tortured, meanwhile dictating his analysis of her demise into his tape player, while Carrie's flash bursts starkly across the ruined building. Meanwhile the audience is aware that the very violence being described by Brian, and implicitly by Carrie, is being barely contained by Early who is savagely fucking Adele in the back of the car (this violence becomes increasingly apparent when Carrie finishes her photography and walks outside and begins to watch Early and Adele fuck, as she watches so Early looks up at leers at her).

This emphasis on the violence of Brian and Carrie's voyeurism is increasingly emphasized by the contrasts and similarities between the two couples. Thus Brian vicariously enjoys Early's violence during the bar room brawl, shooting the gun and the general atmosphere of bravado. Simultaneously Carrie – who finds Early repulsively aggressive in his dominance of Adele – enjoys watching Early fuck Adele (the active/passive dichotomy appears to apply to the sex in which the couple engage). But Carrie can distance herself from the reality of her voyeuristic pleasure by watching the copulation via the camera, similarly when – to her dismay – Brian shoots Early's gun, she shoots with her camera. Carrie's camera, and her relationship to it, thus mirrors the relationship of the male protagonists to the gun (Carrie's voyeurism is specifically linked to her gaze via the camera, through which she can unflinchingly watch and photograph, however when she is held hostage by Early and watches the murder of a police man she turns her head away). Both devices shoot, but while the gun kills, the camera only captures the moment of death and the images of death. In the final eventuality Carrie does not become a killer (although Brian does) however it is Carrie who has most in common with Early (see below).

The killer on the road sub-genre reached its cinematic zenith in Oliver Stone's *Natural Born Killers*, 1994 (which, like *True Romance* was based on a script originally by Tarantino[8], although Tarantino would distance himself from Stone's film upon its release). Even before its theatrical release in Britain the film had something of a cult notoriety in the collective discourses which focused on the text and its relationship to/with contemporary youth culture. The BBFC delayed classifying the film for some time, before demanding several (brief) cuts be made in the (already cut for the MPAA) film before it could be released.

Natural Born Killers follows the murderous spree (fifty-two victims) of white trash husband and wife tag-team-killers Mickey and Mallory Knox. The film opens with the couple having already embarked on their killing spree, and via 'flashback' (stylistically the film deliberately seeks to problematize the traditional war and cinema of film language) the audience gradually becomes aware of the couple's past. Mallory comes from an exceptionally violent family, and has been raped by her fat, disgusting and abusive father since she was a young child. She may even be the mother of her younger brother, a monstrous looking brat with Kiss-style make up adorning his face. One evening, after being groped and threatened by her father, Mallory meets Mickey, who has come to deliver beef to the family home. It is love at first sight, and the two steal Mallory's father's car, for which Mickey is imprisoned on charges of Grand Theft Auto. A freak tornado allows Mickey to escape from the prison ranch and head for Mallory's house (the tornado, of course, being the agent by which Dorothy is removed from home, and consequently must embark on her journey through Oz). Here the couple beat and drown Dad, and burn Mom alive, along – presumably – with the entire house. Mickey and Mallory flee together, while Mallory's brother makes his own escape. Mickey's background is never made completely clear, other than the fact that he witnessed his father's suicide as a child.

On the road Mickey and Mallory create their own marriage, citing their own vows and mixing their blood. Meanwhile a TV show, *American Maniacs*, recounts their rampage down the apocalyptically named Route 666 (a "road to Hell in front of us" states Mickey). Interviews with teenagers around the world reveal that Mickey and Mallory are becoming a cult ("If I was a mass murderer I'd be Mickey and Mallory" says one teen). Cut to a windswept desert town and Mickey and Mallory going to a motel. In the motel the two watch a rapid edit of violent television and film, alongside a natural history program which depicts various animals copulating. As Mickey and Mallory begin to fuck the view from the motel window changes to a rapid edit of stock footage depicting various historical acts of violence, primarily images of Nazis. Mickey is not looking at Mallory while they make love, and the two begin to argue, the problem is that Mickey wants to rape the girl tied up in the corner of the room. Angry, Mallory storms out, finds a teenager, who she persuades to go down on her, before she kills him. Noticeably cut from the film was a violent rape and murder committed by Mickey on his youthful hostage (a cut demanded by the MPAA).

The following day the two run out of gasoline and become lost in the desert. Leaving the car the two walk and argue through the sand until they come to a small homestead. Here they meet a Native American who lets them into his small hut, a fire burns in its centre and a rattle snake sits coiled on the floor. To his grandson the old man states (in his native tongue) that the murderers are "lost in a world of ghosts" and have "sad sickness", both have watched "too much tv". As the old man articulates this so the words are projected across Mickey's and Mallory's chests. The two gun happy lovers fall asleep, but in the middle of the night Mickey wakes from a dream of his youth, and 'accidentally' shoots the elderly man. As Mallory berates him ("Bad. Bad. Bad. Bad. Bad. Bad." she states, poking Mickey in the chest with her forefinger) the dying man reveals that he had seen his own death at the hands of the murderous demon/Mickey Knox in a dream. Mickey and Mallory flee the hut, stealing some petrol on the way. As they walk back to their car tens of rattle snakes appear and snap at their ankles. Both are bitten and have to drive into town for the antidote. At the pharmacist the killers are recognized and the alarm is raised. Mallory is grabbed by sick-boy detective Jack Scagnetti, who wants to rape her, and who uses the threat of "cutting her tits off" to force Mickey to surrender. As Mickey puts his guns down he is savagely beaten by the cops in an oblique reference to the infamous Rodney King video.

The film cuts to a prison, one year later. Here the violent and stupid Governor McClusky has invited Scagnetti to supervise the transfer of the two killers to an asylum for the criminally insane, with the proviso that the two will 'escape' and consequently will have to be 'shot'. The day before this can take place Wayne Gale, the 'auteur' behind *American Maniacs*, will interview Mickey live on air, immediately following the Superbowl. During the interview Mickey – now with a shaven head – refers to Charles Manson as "the king" (Stone stated that much of the interview was inspired by the infamous Geraldo/Manson television interview), as the interview progresses the prison population (portrayed by real convicts) watch in hushed awe, until Mickey states that he is a "Natural Born Killer" and the entire prison explodes in a fury of violence. Mickey grabs a guard's gun and begins to kill guards and tv crew alike, then – while being pursued by Wayne Gale and the few surviving members of his crew – he begins to hunt for Mallory. Meanwhile Mallory is being 'seduced' by Scagnetti in her cell, before he can fuck her she turns and begins to beat and kick Scagnetti. The two fight, suddenly the door is blown open by the rifle-toting Mickey who kills Scagnetti. Aided by a suddenly enthusiastic and murderous Gale the killers escape, although not before watching the prisoners take over the prison.

Finally free the two killers shoot Gale, despite his begging and whingeing, "you always leave a witness" he blubs. Mickey and Mallory point to the camera, which is still broadcasting, "we are" they state, and shoot the journalist. The camera dropped by the journalist films his own demise as the audience watch. The film cuts to the future. Mickey is driving a large truck, in the back Mallory is playing with several children. End.

Natural Born Killers is shot in a variety styles: 35mm, 16mm black and white, super 8, video, stock footage (the second world war, Texas sniper Charles Whitman[9] and even animation). While each style could be used to suggest a 'different' perspective within the text they do not, instead the film is cut – almost at random – to bring the audience into a visually seductive quasi-narcotic rush of images, which create the effect in the audience of a media orgy, as if the entire film is based on the singular pleasure of channel hopping. The free-play of cinematic styles also denies the viewer the chance to maintain a fixed gaze and static mode of identification, instead the viewer is forced into acting as Jean Baudrillard's "pure screen, a switching centre for all the networks of influence"[10]; rather than attempting to become the 'master'[11] of a single gaze, the viewers of Natural Born Killers are forced into the position of a viewing schizophrenia (at one point during the confrontation-cum-interview between Mickey and Wayne Gale the film breaks into an advert for Coke; not only does this appear to be a cynical and audacious example of product placing, the advert also acts as a radical break to any vicarious collective pleasure the audience may experience during this key sequence, like the imaginary audience to Wayne's American Maniacs, we too must 'wait' to see what will happen).

The multiplicity of styles was made possible by director Oliver Stone's utilization of the technological advances of editing, advances which can be used to circumnavigate the traditional linear hands-on style of editing in favour of a high speed computer-based digital edit. The use of such technology enabled an experimentation of editing and styles, and the finished film was "based on editing gut-instinct"[12], and there is – at least according to Stone – no clear narrative perspective delineated by a certain style, so, for example 'reality' is not necessarily perceived in harsh black and white and 'fantasy' is not necessarily depicted via colour. Instead the text deconstructs such 'traditional' markers of 'reality'/'fantasy' by rendering all such cinematic conventions and divisions as ambiguous, removing their traditionally ascribed significations.

Natural Born Killers, like the other films in this sub-genre, is set against an apocalyptic desert landscape – the appropriately named Route 666 – yet the desert, with all its eschatological overtones, is neither the only – or indeed the primary – zone of apocalypse within the film. For much of the film's driving sequences Mickey and Mallory are seen driving against a montage of images, which includes fire, fireworks, television shows and films. The apocalypse is thus played out across the flickering screens of the media, and at the film's opening, immediately following the titles, Mickey articulates this; while they sit in the car, television images of fireworks exploding around them he states "the whole world's comin' to an end, Mal'". The signifier of fire which has marked the sub-genre becomes no longer necessary (despite the burning of Mallory's mother) instead merely its representation on television is enough, it does not need to refer to a real fire but to the simulacrum of fire. In the postmodern society television has replaced the car, no longer do people have to travel in order to see the world, but via television they can experience the world instantaneously without having to leave home. If the modern landscape of the first half of the twentieth century was designed for the car then the postmodern landscape of the late twentieth century has replaced the car with the experience of television, the experience of distance and time (the time needed to travel) becomes burned out in favour of distance and speed (the speed of images across the globe). Mickey and Mallory do not have to travel into the chaos of the space between cities, it is already there on television; existential nausea has been replaced by the giddying effects of multiple images edited in quick succession across the television.

The narrative of Natural Born Killers utilises these television and film images in order to contextualise the crimes of Mickey and Mallory. They are television kids: "TOO MUCH TV" projected across their chests in the desert cabin; Mallory's background is shot on video as a television sit-com à la Father Knows Best, complete with laugh track and knowing asides to the audience. The Knox's media-saturated environment defines their 'reality', more importantly Natural Born Killers suggests that, at least in part, the killer's activities are due to the media, or a result of a media-saturated world which bombards its audience with indiscriminate images of violence (this is emphasized by the motel scene and the barrage of images of sex and violence, which lead up to the sexual violence enacted by Mickey – which was cut from the film – and Mallory, such a glib use of imagery suggests that the film is offering a cause and effect hypothesis for the killers' brutality). In the prison, during a montage of images, we see Frankenstein's monster, a creature created by, but ultimately beyond the control of, humanity. Cutting the monster in among the other television and film footage which bombards the audience draws a direct link between images and the creation of a society. This is again emphasized by the entire television show within the text, *American Maniacs*.

The media glut which defines *Natural Born Killers'* aesthetic acts as an aporia: it allows the audience a multiplicity of perspectives, and radically destabilises the notion of a homogenous textuality in favour of a heterogeneous intertextuality, created via its channel-surfing aesthetic. However the media is also presented in simplistic, and occasionally even naive, terms as 'glorifying' violence and being partly responsible for the breakdown of the social realm which has allowed serial killers to emerge.

This presentation of the media is contrary to the rest of the films in the sub-genre. The earlier films depict the media as having an influence on the killers, from Kit's (and Starkweather's) adolescent identification with James Dean, to Sailor and Clarence's Elvis fixations, but these media figures are rebellious archetypes and are viewed by the protagonists – and the texts – as symbols of rebellion and existential individualism rather than as the reason for the killing spree.

What all these films share is the articulation of the fantasy of being able to escape the repressed violence of the city, of the home and nuclear family, and travel into the chaos and potentiality of the 'beyond', aiming for the utopia of their own Emerald City. The zone outside the cities which becomes repeatedly marked as a place beyond all law (symbolic and legislative), a place where boundaries collapse, and order vanishes to a pin prick in the rearview mirror. In *Badlands* this collapse iterated the psychic state of the protagonists, and especially Kit, whose journey was doomed from the start. However post-*Badlands* the text's central protagonists always return to the symbolic order, thus in *Wild At Heart*, *True Romance* and *Natural Born Killers* the couple, by the end of the film, have 'matured', married and become parents, adopting the traditional values of a monogamous, heterosexual nuclear family. The killers of these films emerge as exceptionally conservative figures, who may annihilate or flee their backgrounds, killing those who dominate them, whether family, landlord or pimp, but who ultimately seek to reproduce these very values within their own lives. *Badlands* is also the only film to expressly articulate the murderer's conservatism, as Malick stated at the time of the film's release:

"(Kit) thinks of himself as a successor to James Dean – a rebel without a cause – when in reality he's more like an Eisenhower conservative. 'Consider the minority opinion', he says into the rich man's tape recorder, 'but try to get along with the majority opinion once it's accepted'. He dosen't really believe any of this, but he envies the people who do, who can. He wants to be like them, like the rich man he locks in the closet, the only man he dosen't kill, the only man he sympathises with, and the one least in need of sympathy. It's not infrequently the people at the bottom who most vigorously defend the very rules that put and keep them there."[13]

Much of this conservatism in the texts post-*Badlands* is reflected in the symbolism of chaos outside the cities; in the urban landscape the characters identity is fixed (thus, for example, Mickey is a delivery man, Early is a janitor, Clarence is a sales assistant) but when the characters leave the safety of the metropolis their identity is thrown into question, consequently much of the journey is about searching for an identity (hence the fixation with rebellious archetypes, whose identity could be easily adapted as one's own in the desert). This search for an identity, which can finally only emerge through the embracing of the Oedipal family, and the arriving at the destination, becomes the central focus of these films. Narrative closure can only be achieved when the serial killer/s are able to fix their identity, until this point they are forced to continue to travel, or – like Early – must die. In *Badlands* this textual closure becomes manifested in the irony of Holly's final deadpan narration; Kit is executed and she marries her lawyer's son, thus her identity – or lack of – is gained through a direct return to the urban and also to a, literal, bonding with the law. However there is no apparent irony in the closure of the other texts.

The most abrupt narrative closure comes in *Kalifornia* via Carrie, who has been identified as sexual – via shots of her in her bra and panties – and simultaneously identified as artistic, independent and strong. Carrie initially appears as an erotic androgen with her skin-tight black clothes and short black hair and she thus must be read as a post-feminist heroine. Like the serial killer she offers a threat to order and raises questions concerning the nature of identity, further Carrie needs to cross the country in order to ascertain her identity, like the murderous boyfriends of *Badlands* and *Natural Born Killers* she inaugurates the journey. However – unlike the killers of the other texts who can fix their identity by the simple repetition of their murderous act – by the film's closure, and her return to the order of the city, Carrie has been forced into her place in the symbolic order. At the film's close she appears in baggy, more easily feminine-identified, clothes, with long hair. More importantly her photography, which originally was rejected because of its explicit eroticism, has now been accepted. Although the film does not depict her new work its title is articulated by Carrie: "Icons". Such a title infers that her new work – rather than challenging the norms of society as her previous work did, via its images of faceless (and hence lacking an identity[14]) blacks and whites engaged in sexual acts – actually embraces the culturally traditional concept of the icon, the biggest icon being – of course – the Virgin Mary, thus the photographic work shifts Carrie from 'whore' to 'virgin'. Carrie thus returns from the journey across country, having been 'punished' for her individualism via her rape at the hands of Early, who expressly articulates his disgust at her erotic photos. Carrie now 'knows' and is 'accepting' her place in the symbolic order.

These few films, then, use the road as a quest for an identity, and the journey's end – and film's close – become the point at which the characters can re-enter the symbolic order. Crucially the films – bar *Badlands* – use an East/West journey across America (the drive undertaken in *Badlands* is also an East/West journey, but it is far more a journey to nowhere). This is a journey which has a culturally specific resonance, because it is a journey historically identified by American society as pioneering, as travelling to a promised land, a new world of opportunity away from the Eurocentrism of the East Coast. The frontier of the American west represents the birth place of the American national identity, thus by journeying west the characters of these films are enacting a culturally specific voyage which seeks to articulate an identity.

Charles Starkweather and Caril Ann Fugate, the couple who 'inspired' these films, remain absent from them, their shadows remain cast across the text but they are blurred, barely recognisable shapes. It is only *Badlands*, with its narrative that echoes the story of Starkweather, which makes any direct reference to his life and crimes. Those other films described here engage with a repetition of cinematic texts, the most central being *Badlands* with its depiction of murderous youth on the run. Even *Natural Born Killers*, with its name-checks to Manson and Whitman amongst others, fails to allude to the Starkweather case directly, despite its conscious engagement with the very concept of rebellious youth. Similarly of all the crimes alluded to in the subplot of *Kalifornia* concerning Brian's book, none even transpire on the road, they are instead oblique iconic references to films such as *The Texas Chainsaw Massacre* etc. Furthermore *Wild At Heart* and *True Romance* both embrace a postmodern pastiche of previous texts, genres and – more importantly – culture, a large number of which come from '50s popular culture; Nicholas Ray's classic film *Johnny Guitar*, Elvis Presley, and '50s retro-style fashion. The '50s represent, at least in these films, a golden age:

"The real high spot for the US ('when things were going on') and you can still feel the nostalgia for those years, for the ecstasy of power, when power held power."[15]

Of course Starkweather was a product of the '50s, for whom these now supposedly 'kitsch' icons were once actual symbols of rebellion. In referring to these icons *Wild At Heart* and *True Romance* reveal yet another narrative gap in which the figure of Charles Starkweather demands to be placed.

Finally, then, these films play with images of alienation and angst, but always resolve the protagonists' dilemmas with a return to the conservatism of 'being' (be it via the mechanisms of an arrival at the destination, or the destruction of the killer). The potentialities of the chaos remain ungrasped. Rebellion is rendered merely as a pastiche of previous rebellious icons. Only *Badlands* fully recognises the killer as victim and, simultaneously, as fundamentally conservative: as a nihilist unable to grasp either the velocity or necessity of his own nihilism. While the other films in this sub-genre offer a spectacle of rebellion that becomes merely another image, without meaning and yet offering the illusion (and believing in the mystique) of depth and authenticity. Meanwhile Starkweather is always present in these texts, but only at their margins, suspended from the narratives which remain haunted by his denim-clad ghost.

NOTES

1. This essay focuses on the mainstream/Hollywood cinema's explorations of road-weary killer couples routed in the Starkweather/Fugate story; however there are other films which owe a noticeable debt to Starkweather/Fugate.

Murder In The Heartland, 1993, directed by Robert Markowitz, is a true crime TV movie which traces the Charles Starkweather and Caril Ann Fugate story, although hardly classifiable as a part of this potential sub-genre with its emphasis on fact and news-real style realism the film is noteworthy for its – general – accuracy (despite a brief foray into sexual violence via the depiction of Starkweather groping a relatively youthful Mrs Ward). The film suggests the hypothesis put forward by Caril's defence that she was an unwilling accomplice, and tried to leave signs describing her predicament and asking for help (including a note which asked for help, originally designed to be left in a dinner bathroom, but instead found on Caril's person by the arresting officer, unfortunately for Caril the note was lost and she was unable to use it in her defence). *Murder In The Heartland* also devotes some considerable time to the trials, and especially Fugate's, and raises many questions regarding Starkweather's contradictory statements concerning Caril's involvement with the crimes. *Murder In The Heartland* falls down, however, with the casting of Tim Roth as the eighteen-year-old Charles Starkweather (this is all the more surprising given that Fairuza Balk, who plays Caril, is exceptionally well cast).

Charles Starkweather and Caril Ann Fugate also strongly influenced the 1963 B-movie classic *The Sadists* (aka *The Profile Of Terror*). Directed by James Landis the film, starring Arch Hall Jr (whose father Arch Hall Sr produced and distributed the movie), focuses on a delinquent couple who "terrorize three smalltown high school teachers whose car has broken down near a deserted garage." (—Charles Beesley, in Michael Weldon, **The Psychotronic Encyclopedia of Film**, Plexus: London, 1989, p.601.) Unfortunately, given the nature of B-movie production in the '60s, and Arch Hall's death in 1979, the location of the film is currently unknown, although it is rumoured that video copies exist.

Finally, in 1986 underground film director Richard Kern produced the sleaziest of all Starkweather-type movies. Entitled *Fingered*, the film, something of a *noir* 8mm epic, follows a violent greaseball and his girlfriend (played by Lydia Lunch), who works as a phone sex employee, as they hit

---

the road. The couple talk dirty, fuck, and drive around California, until they come across a young panic-stricken hitch-hiker, who they attack... [See my *Deathtripping – The Cinema Of Transgression* (Creation Books, 1995) for further details.]

2. There are many films which could be included in this paper; road movies such as Ridley Scott's *Thelma And Louise*, and teen killer films such as *Heathers*, make oblique references to the Starkweather and Fugate case. Yet none of these films engage with the love-on-the-run thematic in the same way as the films included in this essay; thus *Thelma And Louise* is about a couple who become wanted through misfortune rather than nihilism, and *Heathers* is more of an exercise in satirizing the banality of the wealthy teenager than in existential angst.

3. An independent production, written, produced and directed by Malick, and made for $300,000, *Badlands* was brought by Warners for a million dollars.

4. Baudrillard, **America**, p.24.

5. The chaos behind the commonplace is, of course, a regular thematic concern of Lynch, whose *Blue Velvet* similarly exposes the churning Oedipal disorder which lurks beneath the veneer of the all-American small town. What separates *Wild At Heart* from its predecessors is that, while Lynch's earlier films saw a chaos beneath the world, the chaos was contained, it always threatened to submerge the subject but never did. Thus *Blue Velvet*'s central protagonist emerges from the crisis of the primal scenes into a fully Oedipalised subject, and the chaos which threatened to destroy his identity is itself destroyed. Such a successful narrative resolution cannot exist in *Wild At Heart*, a film which can only become optimistic – can only have the 'happy' ending and narrative resolution – via the magic of the Good Witch who appears at the film's climax, the narrative equilibrium which is traditionally restored at the end of Hollywood texts is rendered itself as a parody.

6. Baudrillard, **America**, p.53.

7. Race also remains an issue at the margins of the text. Carrie's photos depict black/white sex scenarios, and when Early, who is identified with the South and thus with the 'negative', finds them he mocks and degrades Carrie for her work but – perhaps surprisingly – ignores the racial element of the pictures.

8. *Natural Born Killers* was Tarantino's second script.

9. Whitman was an architectural engineering student who, on August 1st, 1966, climbed to the top of the bell tower at the University of Texas and, armed with a variety of rifles, began to shoot at passers by. He killed three people – including his wife and mother – before going to the university, here he killed a further eighteen people, before three policemen gunned him down. An autopsy revealed a massive brain tumour pushing onto the aggression centre of his brain.

10. Baudrillard, *The Ecstasy Of Communication*, in Hal Foster, editor, **Postmodern Culture**, Pluto Press: London & Concord, MA, 1990, p.133.

11. Master because, as feminist film theorist Laura Mulvey articulated in her essay *Visual Pleasure And Narrative Fiction*, the Hollywood film text creates a male scopophilic or voyeuristic pleasure. Where Mulvey's work fails is that it assumes cinematic gaze and modes of identification are constructed on a psychoanalytic and gendered basis, Mulvey thus privileges the phallocentric constructed psychoanalytic discourse as a 'truth' discourse.

12. Stone quoted in Smith, *Oliver Stone: Why Do I Have To Provoke?* in **Sight And Sound**, December, 1994, p.12.

13. Walker, *Malick On Badlands* in **Sight And Sound**, Spring 1975, Volume 44, No.2, p.82.

14. Crucially, Early recognises the woman in the photographs as Carrie – hence linking the two figures via their lack of a fixed identity.

15. Baudrillard, **America**, p.107.

Bibliography

Allen, William; **Starkweather: The Story of A Mass Murderer**.
Leyton, Elliot; **Hunting Humans**.
Linna, Miriam; *Starkweather*, **Bad Seed #3**.
Nash, Jay Robert; *A Little World All Our Own*, in **Couples Who Kill**.
O'Donnell, Jeff; **Starkweather: A Story Of Mass Murder On The Great Plains**.
Reinhardt, James M.; **The Murderous Trail Of Charles Starkweather**.
Wilson, Colin and Seaman, Donald; **The Encyclopedia Of Modern Murder, 1962–83**.

Atkinson, Michael; *Crossing The Frontiers*, **Sight And Sound**, Volume 4, issue 1.
Baudrillard, Jean; **America**, trans. Chris Turner.
Baudrillard, Jean; *The Ecstasy Of Communication*, in Hal Foster, editor, **Postmodern Culture**.
Grant, Barry Keith; **Planks Of Reason: Essays On The Horror Film**.
Smith, Gavin; *Oliver Stone: Why Do I Have To Provoke?*, **Sight And Sound**, December 1994.
Virilio, Paul; **The Lost Dimension**.
Walker; *Malick On Badlands*, **Sight And Sound**, Volume 44, issue 2.
Willis, Sharon; *Special Effects: Sexual And Social Difference In Wild At Heart*, **Camera Obscura**, 25/26.

DEATHTRIPPING

The Cinema of Transgression

DEATHTRIPPING

An Illustrated History Of The Cinema Of Transgression

Deathtripping is an illustrated history, account and critique of the "Cinema Of Transgression", providing a long-overdue and comprehensive documentation of this essential modern sub-cultural movement. Including: A brief history of underground/ trash cinema: seminal influences including **Andy Warhol, Jack Smith, George and Mike Kuchar, John Waters**. Interviews with key film-makers, including **Richard Kern, Nick Zedd, Cassandra Stark, Beth B, Tommy Turner**; plus associates such as **Joe Coleman, Lydia Lunch, Lung Leg** and **David Wojnarowicz**. Notes and essays on transgressive cinema, philosophy of transgression; manifestos, screen-plays; film index and bibliography. Heavily illustrated with rare and sometimes disturbing photographs, *Deathtripping* is a unique guide to a style of film-making whose impact and influence can no longer be ignored.

CINEMA   Paperback   1 871592 29 1   256pp   £11.95 • $16.95

you have just read
born bad
a creation book
published by:
creation books
83, clerkenwell road, london ec1r 5ar, uk
tel: 0171-430-9878 fax: 0171-242-5527
creation books is an independent publishing organisation producing
fiction and non-fiction genre books of interest to a young, literate
and informed readership.
*creation products should be available in all proper bookstores; please
ask your uk bookseller to order from:*
turnaround, 27 horsell road, london n5 1xl
tel: 0171-609-7836 fax: 0171-700-1205
non-book trade and mail order:
ak distribution, 22 lutton place, edinburgh eh8 9pe
tel: 0131-667-1507 fax: 0131-662-9594
readers in europe please order from:
turnaround distribution, 27 horsell road, london n5 1xl
tel: 0171-609-7836 fax: 0171-700-1205
readers in the usa please order from:
subterranean company, box 160, 265 south 5th street, monroe, or
97456
tel: 503 847-5274 fax: 503-847-6018
non-book trade and mail order:
ak press, po box 40682, san francisco, ca 94140-0682
tel: 415-923-1429 fax: 415-923-0607
readers in canada please order from:
marginal distribution, unit 102, 277 george street, n. peterborough,
ontario k9j 3g9
tel/fax: 705-745-2326
readers in australia and new zealand please order from:
peribo pty ltd, 58 beaumont road, mount kuring-gai, nsw 2080
tel: 02-457-0011 fax: 02-457-0022
readers in japan please order from:
charles e. tuttle company, 21-13 seki 1-chome, tama-ku, kawasaki,
kanagawa 214
tel: 044-833-1924 fax: 044-833-7559
readers in the rest of the world, or any readers having difficulty in
obtaining creation products, please order direct (+ 10% postage in
the uk, 20% postage outside uk) from our head office
a full catalogue is available on request.